THE ROAD TO WILDCAT

THE LIBRARY
OF ALABAMA
CLASSICS

THE ROAD TO WILDCAT
A Tale of Mountain Alabama

ELEANOR DE LA VERGNE RISLEY

Introduction by Carroll Viera

The University of Alabama Press
Tuscaloosa

Copyright © 2004
The University of Alabama Press
Tuscaloosa, Alabama 35487-0380
All rights reserved
Manufactured in the United States of America

Originally published serially in the Atlantic Monthly in 1928 and
1929 and then in book form by Little, Brown, and Company in 1930.

∞

The paper on which this book is printed meets the minimum re-
quirements of American National Standard for Information Science–
Permanence of Paper for Printed Library Materials, ANSI Z39.48-
1984.

Library of Congress Cataloging-in-Publication Data

Risley, Eleanor De La Vergne, 1867–1945.
The road to Wildcat : a tale of mountain Alabama / Eleanor De La
Vergne Risley ; introduction by Carroll Viera.
    p. cm.
"Originally published serially in the Atlantic Monthly in 1928 and
1929 and then in book form by Little, Brown, and Company in
1930"—T.p. verso.
ISBN 0-8173-5093-4 (pbk. : alk. paper)
1. Alabama—Description and travel. 2. Risley, Eleanor De La Vergne,
1867–1945—Travel—Alabama. 3. Mountain life—Alabama—History—20th century. 4. Mountain people—Alabama—Social life and
customs—20th century. 5. Alabama—Social life and customs—20th
century. I. Viera, Carroll, 1942–II. Title.
F326 .R58 2004 917.6'1063—dc22   2003018417

To
FRANCES POPE WESTON

*who encouraged us to fare forth with a push-
cart; who presented Sisyphus with many
comforts and conveniences; and for whose
entertainment, in lonely mountain camps,
these stories were commenced — to her,
Peter, John, Sisyphus, and I affectionately
dedicate this account of our journey.*

CONTENTS

INTRODUCTION

Carroll Viera

The Road to Wildcat recounts the travels in North Alabama in the mid-1920s of Eleanor Risley; her new husband, Pièrre, referred to as "Peter" in the travelogue; and their dog, John. Published in segments in 1928 and 1929 in the *Atlantic Monthly* and then reorganized and reissued in book form in 1930, this account tells of a remarkable woman whose ideas were far ahead of those of most of her contemporaries and who provides astute reflections on southern mountain life in the early twentieth century.

Limited definitive biographical information is available on Eleanor Risley. Sources include a few short entries in biographical directories, an article in the *Arkansas Gazette* that was based on an interview, the memories of a cousin, and biographical comments from her own writing. Some of this material is contradictory, and Risley seems to have taken occasional poetic license with her own nonfiction, altering names of places and people, for example.

Risley was born in Nashville, Tennessee, in January 1867 (incorrectly listed as 1876 in two minor biographical directories). She died in 1945 during World War II at the age of 78. Her parents were apparently sophisticated and well educated. Her father was Philip Stanton Doss, an attorney who died when his daughter was very young. Her mother, Anne de la Vergne, claimed two distinguished ancestors: Marie Madeleine Pioche de la Vergne, Comtesse de la

Fayette, the seventeenth-century author of *La Princesse de Cléves* (often considered the first great French novel) and a forefather who accompanied the famous French Marquis de Lafayette to America, married a Quaker woman, and joined other immigrant families in operating a woolen mill up the Hudson River from New York.

When still a young girl, Eleanor Risley moved to Henry County, Missouri, where she grew up and spent much of her time with her grandparents and the children of their six sons and two daughters. One of her cousins, who knew her during their childhood and with whom she established a lifelong friendship, was Louis Freund, an artist with the Works Progress Administration (WPA). Freund provided the sketch that accompanies Katharine Murdock Davis's feature article on Risley, based on a personal interview and published in 1911 in the *Arkansas Gazette*. Davis reports that Risley attended a Presbyterian school for girls and then married a Kansas City businessman who, according to Freund, belonged to a prominent Missouri family. Risley and her first husband were parents of one child, Eugene, who seemed to have inherited his mother's artistic flair. In one of her rare allusions to him she recalls that, under her encouragement, he "was forever painting Eves and Aphrodites." Following Eugene's death at age eight, the couple divorced, a common occurrence after the death of a child, though Freund recalls that Risley also disliked the social life of the city.

Following her divorce, Risley spent about two years in San Francisco, where she remarried. Her second husband, Allen Douglas Risley, disappeared and was believed to have drowned. In her book *An Abandoned Orchard*, published in 1932, Risley describes herself as "sorrow-dazed" and "impoverished" during her time in California. The deaths of her child and her second husband must have weighed heavily on her and accounted for her depressed spirits. Her accounts of later times reflect a cheerful and humorous tone, a trait praised by her contemporary reviewers. The scarcity and vagueness of her references to Eugene, whom she never identifies as her son, perhaps indicate an attempt to repress the heartache brought on by his death.

In San Francisco, Risley worked in a number of capacities: as a social worker under the direction of the mother of William Randolph Hearst, as a music teacher, as a musician playing for the movies, and as the researcher for an author working on a book about epilepsy. In the opening chapter of *An Abandoned Orchard*, Risley describes her dreary life in the city, where she lived at a YWCA with three roommates. Too impoverished to enjoy the amenities of city life, she returned to the Midwest and the inheritance of a hundred-acre apple orchard with an additional rocky acreage.

As an orchard owner, she performed her work with an independence and determination that are reflected in all of her writing. During this time she married her third husband, Pièrre Risley, a socialist who had attempted to organize a strike among her workers. Pièrre was unrelated to Risley's second husband, who shared the same surname.

Risley and her third husband became residents of Fairhope, Alabama, where she enjoyed some success as a literary figure. From 1921 to 1924, she contributed written sketches of interesting personalities to the *Fairhope Courier,* which were then collected and reissued as *Real Fairhope Folks* (1928), in a printing of 500 copies. This small volume, in addition to articles about local residents, included two poems and a vignette of a dog.

Risley was diabetic and Pièrre asthmatic. Early in their marriage and warned that she might die within a year, they departed from Fairhope on a vigorous walking tour of the North Alabama mountains in order to improve their health. Risley's accounts of their travels originated in letters to friends. These accounts came to the attention of Ellery Sedgwick, the editor of the *Atlantic Monthly,* who published them serially.

Risley's North Alabama travels with Pièrre during the 1920s were truly remarkable. Maintaining a flexible itinerary, Risley recalls "drifting before the wind of destiny, we ever chose the most unfrequented way." In their mountain trek, long before backpacking became popular, the couple sought out small rural settlements and colorful mountain residents in an adventure that anticipates the more recent backroads travels such as those of Peter Jenkins *(Walk Across America)* and William Least Heat-Moon *(Blue Highways).* Due to altered place names, exact locations that the Risleys visited cannot be identified. Most were remote communities, where strangers were often regarded with suspicion.

Though not a college graduate, Risley was literary, cultivated, and sophisticated. She wrote for an educated readership, using frequent literary, Biblical, and historical allusions; but her text can be understood without a familiarity with these allusions. For example, the Risleys carried their gear in a homemade pushcart named Sisyphus, a name whose significance would elude readers unfamiliar with classical mythology. Risley's prose is also characterized by a flowery style popular among early twentieth-century readers but considered inflated and even ostentatious by twenty-first-century critics. The following passage is typical:"Even in the cool mountains nature makes obeisance to the sun at noonday. The singing birds are already hiding in lost green glades, and the jeweled lizard, forever darting across the white sand, sleeps now, beneath his broad life, as still as the pebble beside him."

Risley's sometimes lofty tone decreases in her descriptions of her interaction with the mountaineers, most of whom responded to her with warmth. She often played her violin for an appreciative audience, listened intently to the mountaineers' stories, and joined congregations in rural church services. Her extroverted personality is suggested by her buoyant tone and energetic style. Her experience as a social worker undoubtedly prepared her for the ease with which she participated in the activities of the mountaineers and laid the foundation for her perceptive observations of early twentieth-century rural Alabama life.

Risley's cast of Alabamians includes an assortment

of bizarre people, including corrupt law enforcement officials, suspicious moonshiners, snake handlers, and thieves; and her experiences were not always idyllic. On one occasion Risley became dangerously ill from accidentally ingesting John's mange medicine, on another she and Pièrre arrived in a valley town penniless after she mistook the wrapper of their traveler's checks for the last check, and on still another the couple was escorted out of the settlement of Wildcat by three armed employees of the local moonshine king. Undaunted by these perils, the Risleys never lost their adventurous spirit.

Nowhere is Risley's unassuming manner better reflected than in her response to fundamentalist religion, a defining feature of the rural South. She hears one mountaineer attest to having been the recipient of faith healing; she listens to another explain the conflict between Apostolics (or Holy Rollers) and Hard Shell Baptists, and she nervously witnesses another demonstrate his faith by handling a rattlesnake before his congregation. She attends a Sacred Harp sing, based upon a four-note musical system that its practitioners traced to Jesus' disciples at the Pentecost, meets a young fiddler whose mother allowed him to play only church tunes, and observes river baptisms.

Though freethinkers, she and Pièrre always respected the genuine piety of the mountaineers. On one occasion, despite his confession that he was weary of preachers, Pièrre even adopted the local dialect to support a mountaineer in a debate with an arrogant evolutionist. Self-righteousness, however, evokes an entirely different response. When a city preacher drives them away from a country revival, Eleanor Risley recalls the retreat of the Moors before murderous Christians. Here and elsewhere, she exposes and denounces arrogance, hypocrisy, greed, and deceit wherever she finds it.

Other social concerns further reflect Risley's political liberalism. A civil libertarian, she recalls, in a manner reminiscent of Thoreau's "Civil Disobedience," her arrest for refusing to pay an exorbitant fee for a city license on a cart of her apples. She briefly alludes to "sordid Birmingham, where thousands walk the streets unemployed," she denounces Southern laws on miscegenation, and she empathizes with the Alabama Cherokee and impoverished mill workers whose families sometimes died from lack of good medical care.

Greed, hypocrisy, and dishonesty, Risley found, were often fueled by the conditions of Prohibition. The corrupt sheriff described in the chapter "Alabama, Here we Rest" is one of her most unsavory characters, with his monopoly on illegal liquor in the county, his absorption or burning of his competitors' businesses, and his enlargement of his chain gang by having his associates plant liquor on unsuspecting victims. Two years after *The Road to Wildcat* was published in book form, the Alabama legislature took action to correct the problem; Risley's work has been credited as a leading cause of this reform. Her account of Wildcat illustrated the corruption of an entire community through the production of moonshine. The prevalence of bootlegging often made the residents in places not often frequented by outsiders suspect the Risleys were revenue officers. Oral tradition has strong roots in the Appalachian Mountains, and *The Road to Wildcat* is filled with stories told to the Risleys by the mountaineers in their own words. Early reviewers noted her use of mountain dialect but disagreed upon the extent of its authenticity. A reviewer for the *Saturday Review of Literature*, for example, praised the dialect as "effective," while a colleague at the *New York Times* suggested that it was "overdone." But while a trained linguist might easily detect inconsistencies and inaccuracies, Eleanor Risley's representation gives a reasonable portrait of the mountain speech for the general reader, for whom the book was intended.

Risley shows remarkable independence and deserves recognition for confident feminism and liberalism rare among Southern women writers of her time. Despite her and Pièrre's ill health, she rarely mentions their condition, though on one difficult occasion she anticipates that "to one of us this journey meant not only an escape from the world, but a last good-bye to earth" and thinks of death as "Dust to dust. No more the dear close kinship with the earth, whatever star the eye of faith may discern in the impenetrable darkness beyond."

Such bleak meditations are rare, however, for a positive tone and an adventurous spirit dominate the travelogue. Throughout her work, Risley vividly portrays a way of life that has largely faded away—men gathering for checkers before a wood stove in country stores which also serve as post offices; women wearing sunbonnets who walk two miles into town to sell eggs; mountain residents who set aside their suspicions to share their homes and their stories with strangers.

Some time after their North Alabama excursion, the Risleys concluded that they could no longer afford to live in Fairhope. In 1926 they relocated to a rural Arkansas community near Ink in Polk County, living in an unpainted cabin on the Ouachita River and sometimes selling eggs and chickens in the town of Mena. When Louis Freund purchased Carrie Nation's last home, Hatchet Hall, to save it from destruction, he invited the Risleys to join his family in Eureka Springs to serve as caretakers in this fourteen-room residence. The couple lived in Hatchet Hall for five years. Then, as now, Eureka Springs was known as a center for eccentric residents and unconventional artists, craftsmen, and free thinkers. Risley's last years must have been gratifying, for in Eureka Springs she was surrounded by people of like minds, enjoyed some acclaim as a writer, and was free of poverty. Younger writers often visited her seeking advice.

Following a stroke, Pièrre passed away in 1943. Two years later, Risley underwent surgery in the General Hospital at Little Rock for a broken hip, slipped into a coma, and died. She left no direct descendants.

Risley's other published works also provide interesting reading. The special collections division of the University of Arkansas library houses some of her unpublished writings, but none of these works better represent their remarkable creator than *The Road to Wildcat.*

THE ROAD TO WILDCAT

I

SNAKE NIGHT UP POSEY HOLLER

JOHN and I were resting by the wayside. We could hear behind us the rattle of our Chinese wheelbarrow which Peter pushed along the rocky path. John, our beloved mongrel, who just missed being a setter, lapped delicately the water from one of the hundreds of crystal springs that flickered in the sunlight across the lonely road. The deep maroon of the high bank before us was traced with the buff of honeysuckle bloom and starred with the violet of passion vines. And from the green tangle beyond, the mountain breeze wafted to us that most intoxicating of all perfumes, the fragrance of the wild-grape bloom.

Sisyphus, commonly called Sis, is the name of our pushcart. The day before we started on our journey I stole out and painted the name in great white letters on the green galvanized sides — "Sisy" on

one side and "-phus" on the other, as a constant re-
minder to Peter of his folly in refusing a pack burro for
our months of wandering in the Alabama mountains.

While I was firmly in favor of a donkey, Peter as
firmly scouted the very thought of this "short and
simple animal of the poor." Down through the
mists of time, working, I thought, quite unfairly
through bypaths of asinine history, he asserted that
even Balaam's ass, undoubtedly the best of his race,
had not that blithe and adventurous spirit we desired
in a summer companion. With veiled allusions to
Titania, to Sancho Panza, and R. L. S.'s Modestine,
he ended triumphantly with the symbol of the
political party to which I belong by inheritance.
Proving at last, even to me, that a donkey, while
amiable and well-meaning, is a garrulous, erratic,
unreliable, and expensive animal.

"Now, not exactly a pushcart," he said; "but the
kind of wheelbarrow which I shall design and con-
struct will not wander about and bray at night.
Moreover, it will be a little house that we carry with
us always — like a snail, you know."

"Very well," I sighed. "But it shall be upon your
own head. You are the snail. But a pushcart!"

"It's a wheelbarrow! Why, da Vinci invented
the — er — vehicle."

So with immense pride Peter built a green galvanized cart with one front bicycle wheel and two back
ones, a wide bar across the back so that we could
both push when necessary, and even a little harness

in front where John could pull if we were ever in dire
need and had to proceed at a snail's pace.

On May day we boarded the Jonquil — the John
Quill — and steamed up the Alabama River, Sisyphus, John, Peter, and I, past the uninviting black
lands. Leisurely days watching the nimble negroes
at the villages pile the Jonquil with incredible bur-
dens of wood; answering the questions of farmers
about Sisyphus; and landing, sometimes, with John
for exercise. For John was imprisoned in a special
hades below. And almost every negro who passed
would say: "Yas 'm. Thet 's a mighty fine dawg.
I jes' give him a bone. But I reckon you-all 'll have
to come down an' O.K. it. He won't eat nothin'
'ithout it 's O.K.'d." And after the expected tip, I
would seek John in his misery and find him completely barricaded with bones which he would refuse
to touch unless O.K.'d. But I reminded him that
three days of purgatory is a small slice in a dog's life
for four months of heaven. And one happy day we
landed at a little town and set out for the foothills
of the mountains.

Now for weeks we had reveled in the freedom I had
almost despaired of finding before bidding good-bye
to the friendly earth. Weeks of bliss, wandering
down dim, beckoning roads, sleeping on the ground
with pebbles in our backs, learning to glide like
Indians with no lost motion, gaining strength daily
from the stern old mother of us all. Camping for
hours or for days beside a singing stream. Con-

sulting our road map with feverish delight for some especially remote spot, and then carelessly wandering down quite another alluring path. Selecting, purely for its quaint or romantic name, some place on the map where our mail should be sent, and finding it an almost inaccessible little cage on a mountain top.

Strenuous sometimes, — this belated wedding journey in double harness, — and dangerous sometimes among the moonshiners ever on the watch for "informers."

From tales heard at the feet of my elders I knew that somewhere on an isolated mountain top my great-grandfather slept. And that somewhere among these simple people that he had learned to respect and admire, his house and that of his relative, a famous portrait painter of that day, might still be found.

Not that we especially cared to find my great-grandfather's tomb. But we found that such an avowed intention provided us with a somewhat convenient *raison d'être*. A laudable ambition to seek your great-grandfather's tomb is more acceptable even to your best friend than pushing a wheelbarrow up a mountain for the sheer love of it.

In the high rock's shadow, among the ferns and galax leaves, bubbled an icy spring. I leaned against a sweet-gum tree, and waited for the water to boil on our little camp fire, while Peter shucked the sweet

corn with which Sisyphus was loaded. John pawed
frantically at a cool cellar he was digging in the soft
earth. For it was hot — high noon by my wrist
watch. And though we had loitered on the way, we
had pushed the cart up and up the mountain since
sunrise in the valley below.

A woman wearing a glistening white sunbonnet
crossed the road from the log cabin opposite. She
carried a covered dish which she gave to me and
said : —

"We-all had fried apple pies fur dinner, and I
brung some over. I 'd be proud if you-all 'd take
'em."

We thanked her, and she sat on a stone against the
rough brown rock where the passion vine climbed,
and carefully removed her immaculate bonnet. We
were startled by her beauty. Even John stopped
digging for a moment. Young, but serene and
stately, with chiseled features and a skin of nacre,
she smiled there, a mountain flower, sturdy but very
lovely. The faded lavender of her sleeveless apron-
dress, where the shadows of the passion vine fell
in faint green filigree, draped her firm body with
enchanting grace.

She asked no questions, for the mountain woman
is punctiliously polite. But as we talked of the
weather, the roads, and the cotton, Peter's eyes met
mine, and I knew that we both felt that here was
more than the mere beauty of a wild flower. For
while there was no hint of condescension at our home-

less state, — a mountaineer loves above everything his home, and can conceive no reason for leaving it, other than being thrust out by misfortune, — there was in her manner a curious air of gentle importance; and her words, commonplace enough, bore a strange balm of other-whereness, as though she spoke from a height afar off.

When dinner was served on Sis's tin top, she rose and said: "When you-all belong to go on, stop by. I'd love to give you some gyarden truck. Jest onions, and sweet corn, and some English peas. We hain't got a great chance of a gyarden, fur my man is away loggin', and we got hit all to do. My chillern is jest eleven and twelve yars old."

We thanked her and told her we should start on at once after dinner and would stop by; and we watched her curiously as she disappeared in the "dogtrot," or open hall, of her house. After dinner Peter solemnly produced our last tailor-made cigarette, and divided it exactly. I knew this meant a rare occasion, and that after the last precious puff there was speculative thought ahead. For the home-grown tobacco of the mountains is potent. One cool, rainy day I sat before the fireplace with a madonna who rocked a moonshiner's infant of two weeks and chewed incessantly. When she offered me a chew and I refused it her face fell. So, in a social effort, I dried a leaf before the flame and rolled a cigarette. In a rapidly revolving room I was able to reach the bed in the nearest corner. Peter came in, and the madonna said, "Stranger, I hain't got nothin' but gal tobacco, but if you 'll reach up on that high shelf thar, they 's some good." I waved a feeble warning from the bed, but Peter rushed upon his fate, and presently rushed out again.

When the last puff of smoke, upheld by a sharpened match, had vanished, I said, "Did you observe how gently she spoke to us, as if we were orphan children astray?" "Yes," answered Peter, "that beautiful being feels superior to us. It 's not her beauty. She seems unconscious of that. Perhaps we 'll solve the mystery at the house. She may have a mail-order carpet, or a cottage organ."

We found in the poor cabin the same exquisite neatness and air of serenity that surrounded the woman herself. The children were in the cotton field, but she had gathered the peas and onions, and had added a pound of dewy butter from the well. As we left I said, "You must be very happy here; you seem to enjoy being kind." "Yes," she replied, "I am. — No," to Peter, "I don't want no money. The onliest reason I hain't plumb happy is because I don't live whar I kin see more folks to holp. I have been healed of pellágra by prayer, and I owes the Lord a heap o' thanks."

I sat down on the doorstone, and Peter rolled Sis into the shade at the same instant.

She went on: "Hit war two yars ago that the Apostolics war a-holdin' a big meetin' over thar by the spring."

"Apostolics?" asked Peter.

"Some folks call 'em Holy Rollers. I war so bad I could n't go. My man war away loggin', but Pappy and the chillern went. So they heerd about me, and fur seven days they prayed fur me. Nary minute o' the time, night ner day, some of 'em was n't on their knees. I did n't believe much in 'em, but Pappy did. I could n't use my hands any more. The flesh war a-droppin' off. I jest set in the room in the big chur most o' the time. The seventh day I war a-settin' thar readin' my Bible — I kin read print. Hit war jest sundown, and the room war all full o' red light. All at oncet I riz up and said, 'Pappy, I 'm healed!' and I walked over to Pappy, and that night we all went to meetin' — Pappy, and me, and the chillern. And I 'm so well, and so full o' thanks, hit seems I cain't do enough fur the Lord."

"And your hands! They are beautiful. Not a scar," I cried.

"They healed up right away, and I hain't had a day's sickness sence. I kin work harder 'n ever. Our church thinks hit 's a sin not to keep clean and red up in the house and outside. The neighbors is Hard Shells round here, and they don't like the Apostolics."

"Hard Shells?" I asked, though I knew.

"Hard Shell Baptists. But they 'll all tell you I war healed jest like that. I wish I could go to the big meetin' they 're a-holdin' up Posey Holler —

hit's too fur. Hit'll run two weeks yit. But maybe you-all's started thar?"

"Yes," I said quickly, distrusting the masculine mind in the uptake, "that is where we are going."

This was news to Peter, but he caught himself in time and did n't say so.

"I hate to tell you-all, but you're in danger fur the next mile. I'd go with you-all, but hit would n't holp none. They knows I'm a Apostolic, and agin liquor. Hit's this-a-way. The Gulf is jest on yer left hand and —"

"What is the Gulf?" asked Peter.

"Hit's a great big valley over a steep bluff whar nobody goes but them as is hidin' from the sheriff. Thar's bars, and rattlers, and copperheads in hit. And stills all over the aidge of hit. Hit's a awful dark place full o' trees and vines till you cain't git through hardly. And they's a deep river runnin' through hit whar they don't dare fish, fur the cottonmouths is thar by the hundreds."

"And that," I murmured feebly, "is on our left! What, then, is on our right?"

"Moonshiners. The first house is whar the biggest of 'em all lives. He leads 'em all. They jest whooped a boy and sent him outen the county, accusin' him of bein' a informer. His maw lives the next house. She's a widder woman. If you gits past that mile you-all'll come out on Happy Top whar old Uncle Tutweiler lives. He is rich. He hain't no moonshiner, but they lets him alone.

Uncle Tut hain't a church member, but he air a good man."

"And it 's a mile of that!" said Peter.

"Yes, a full mile. Mister, you let your woman walk on in front. Nary a man in these mountings 'd hurt a woman. But ef you war ahead, they might whoop you, or shoot from behind a rock, thinkin' you war a informer."

We thanked her and said good-bye. Suddenly she turned. "I 'll git on my knees and pray fur you past that mile. I 'd be proud if you-all 'd write to me how you gits along and about the big meetin'. My name is Laura Scott, and my boy kin read writin' a little." (And penciled letters have come to us — scrawled accounts of weather and crops — that bear to us another message than the ill-spelled words convey.)

In silence we tied John securely to the cart. I carried the rifle, and we walked abreast. Before the fearsome house at the right sat a gigantic man in a chair propped against the wall. He stared a moment, and we saw him run to the dogtrot and take his rifle from a rack on the wall and disappear into the house. I dropped behind, but we walked steadily on. Presently we were in front of the cabin of the "widder woman" whose son had been "whooped" and run "outen the county." Ripe peaches had fallen over the stone wall of the yard, and we stopped a moment to pick them up. Death might be approaching from the rear, but peaches are peaches. A woman called from the dogtrot and ran out with a dasket of peaches and two knives, and we sat on the stone wall and ate the fruit. The woman was old and unkempt, and though her words were kindly her voice held but one tone, that of acid bitterness, as though life had drained her of all but one emotion. The voices of the mountain women are all monotonous, including perhaps but three tones at best. But this voice was like the sad twanging of a single low-pitched string.

I said, "The house we passed a while back. The woman told us of her healing. Do you know of it?"

"Yes, she tells everybody. She 'lows she ort to."

"But it's true?" asked Peter.

"Yes, hit's true. Prayer is prayer. But I hain't got no use fur the folks that done the prayin'. Them Holy Rollers a-pettin' copperheads and rattlers! The way I'd please God is to smash 'em with a rock! Them Holy Rollers is havin' a big meetin' up Posey Holler. To-morrow's snake night."

"Snake night?" I quavered.

"Yes, hit's Sunday night and they brings in a rattler and pets him. Thar'll be a big crowd. Some of 'em'll git bit like the feller that died last week on tother mounting. Temptin' the Lord like that! They 'lowed he wasn't under the Power when he was bit or 't wouldn't a hurted him. I hyar they is more careful now. They says they feels hit when the Power comes, like wind over 'em. Pity hit don't blow their haids offen 'em, temptin' God like that!"

Down the road came six gaunt mountaineers, walking abreast, each bearing a rifle on his shoulder. I grasped the stone wall firmly, resolved to remain there indefinitely. But the woman rose quickly and said, "You-all best putt the peaches in your little wagon and go on. Hit won't do you ner me no good fur 'em to see you hyar. They mighty nigh killed my boy tother day. They might take you-all fur informers." And with a frightened air she ran through the dogtrot, where she took a gun from the wall, and disappeared in the house.

We walked on. The road was clear for a way. But soon we came to a sharp turn which led down to a thicket of laurel under dense trees. "Here," I said, "is where I walk on ahead."

Peter demurred and insisted on leaving me with the cart, and walking on with John and the rifle. But there was a woman praying for me in a cabin back there, and I choked out good-bye, and ran down the road with the rifle.

The steep rocky way led down to a sullen stream stealing its course to the Gulf, where the cottonmouths crawled by hundreds. The loneliness and the silence of the sinister place so oppressed me that it was a relief to see, seated on a great rock which jutted over the water, six men with their rifles across their knees. I called at once, in a voice that did not sound like mine: "I came on ahead to try to shoot a rabbit. Are there any rabbits about here? We are on our way to Uncle

Tutweiler's. This is the right road to Uncle Tut's, is n't it?"

"Yes," answered the gigantic leader of the moonshiners, "and you won't find no rabbit." And they filed down a path by the dark stream. I sat on a fallen tree. I could n't stand. And soon I heard the rattle of the cart, and Peter and John came running down to the ford. We took off our shoes and stockings and carried Sis across the water. I was always hampered by my skirt; but I feared to offend the mountaineers by wearing knickers. Often I have seen mountain women ploughing in flapping skirts.

It seemed a long way to sanctuary, for a mountain mile is not as other miles. But at last there was Happy Top, and Uncle Tutweiler's house. It was an old house. Uncle Tut told me afterward that it had been built almost a century ago. It was made of four large whitewashed log houses joined together in a row with several lean-tos in the rear. Surrounding the front and sides was a rude gallery supported by pillars of great cedars with the limbs left on, where hung saddles and bridles and wearing apparel and baskets of fruit — anything. The cedar posts, polished by vanished hands, were beautiful with the patina of a hundred years, and gleamed like silver in the afternoon sun.

The grapevine telegraph had announced our coming, — perhaps the six moonshiners themselves, — and Uncle Tut, his portly wife, and six stalwart

sons were on the gallery to welcome us. Uncle Tut
was a cripple, — a twisted leg, — but he would have
been a commanding figure anywhere. Tall and lank,
with a hawklike face and a noble forehead, he looked
every inch the leader of his tribe. King Tut indeed!

Peter asked permission to put up our little tent
near the house, and Mrs. Tut took me into "the
room." "The room" marks the aristocracy of the
mountains. It is a living room, though it usually
contains a few snowy beds. This room boasted two
old four-poster beds and two much-carved cottage
organs opposite each other. The walls were hung
with fiddles, banjos, guitars, and a whole row of
harmonicas — or French harps, as they are called.

We declined the cordial invitation to supper, and
after the last of our fried pies, with a grace over
them which I hope reached their donor, we went to
the house, which was rapidly filling with people from
every direction. One frail little woman had walked
four miles, carrying her baby. She showed me her
hands, blistered from chopping cotton all day.

The "music" came down from the wall, and what
an evening we had! Seeing so many fiddles, I left
mine with Sis, and presided at one of the organs. A
returned soldier played the other. They were only
a fraction of a tone apart! We played "Billy in the
Low Ground," "Devil's Dream," "Big Tater in the
Sand," "Black Satin," "Lorena," and sang war
songs and old hymns and late jazz from the Sunday
School books. At midnight, after a rousing "God

Be With You Till We Meet Again," we went happily
to sleep, to wake at dawn and set out for the "big
meetin'" and snake night at Posey Holler.

Uncle Tut said, "Hit 'll be hard fur you-all to find
the way. But I reckon you won't keer ef you do git
lost. You-all 'pear to be jest wanderin'. But Bud
Hall 's jest rid by on his mule goin' up sparkin' to
Piney Hill Church. You-all foller his tracks. Hit 's
a little to the left, and hit 's the only water you-all 'll
find. Stop thar fur dinner. They 'll tell you frum
thar on. Posey Holler runs right up to the top o'
Milksick Mounting."

"Milksick!" I said. "What a name!"

"Yes, the gover'mint tries to keep hit fenced off.
Hit 's got a pizen weed that makes cows and folks
sick. Far'well! I wisht you-all could stop longer."

It was a slow climb. Sometimes we lost Bud
Hall's track and wandered into logging roads and
cow paths. And Peter was in a desperate hurry.
As we left, Mrs. Tut had presented us with six varie-
ties of sweet apples and a live chicken, and, while
Sis still bore sweet corn, he was determined on
chicken à la Maryland for dinner. At last, arrived
at the little unpainted church, we pushed the cart
into the brush arbor before it, and Peter started a
fire. But an old man appeared from the church and
said, "Stranger, this is God's house, and everybody 's
welcome. You-all come right in to Sunday School.
I 'm leadin' to-day on 'Go ye into all the world and
preach the gospel.'"

I murmured something about our appearance —
. that we should like to freshen up a bit, but the leader
said at once, "Come right in like you air! God says
the pore is always with us."

Peter cast a regretful glance at the chicken, but we
followed the good man into the church, separating at
the door, for it is a scandal for the sexes to sit together
in a church. It is n't done. The leader took Peter
into his Bible class, and Peter told me afterward
there were only two men in the class who could read,
and they word by word like children. But the Bible
was passed to each to read a verse. As he passed
the Book, each man would say, "I left my specs at
home to-day." Peter began to fear the country was
given over to ophthalmia, when he caught a twinkle
in the leader's eye. But he so far outdid himself
that he was asked to make an address after the
lesson, which he did with surprising eloquence, on
the subject of foreign missions, making at once a
theatrical exit "centre door, fancy," as the old
actors used to say, pretending there was something
wrong at the cart. I knew it was the chicken prey-
ing upon his mind, so remained to hear a discussion
in regard to a proposed singing class.

A young mountaineer arose and announced that he
wished to teach "rudimints to the whole settlemint
fur ten nights fur the sum of thirty dollars." He
was a handsome youth, with the jetty hair, the
straight features, and the hall mark of the mountaineer — the snowy forehead above the bronze

below the mark of his hat. I believe a mountain man sleeps in his hat. I have never seen one in a detached state but in a church. Then he sits some time before removing it, shamefacedly, as if a duty to God, but reluctantly, as though parting with an article of his clothing really demanded by a fastidious public.

Now one of the elders arose and objected to the price asked for the lessons. He said they could "git a teacher from over Push Mounting" who would come a whole two weeks for twenty-five dollars. The candidate arose and spoke with some warmth. He said, "I hain't castin' no slurs on no man's rudimints, but I know that man hain't never been offen Push Mounting. *My* rudimints is as good as any man's, fur I spent nine dollars fur my music education, besides five dollars I spent fur board in town gittin' it! And I claim I ort to git more."

At this a stalwart man arose and said, "I hain't objectin' to the price. But I never seen no singing class that wasn't jest a sparkin' school, and I'm agin hit," and sat down. The candidate replied that there would be no sparking at his school. He knowed how to stop it, and he would! At last a visitor from the Valley proposed it be referred to a committee. It was, and we rose and sang "Which Side Air Ye Fightin' On?" and the leader raised his hand for the benediction. I saw his face lengthen and pale as he stared out the open door opposite. I turned to see Peter looking very disreputable, endeavoring to con-

ceal the fact that he was picking a chicken. I
hastened to speak to the leader and incidentally to
tell him that Uncle Tut of Happy Top had presented
us with a chicken. The color came back to his face.
It is one thing to welcome the poor to God's house,
but another to trust them in the matter of a spring
chicken; and the leader's flock was next door to the
church.

It was dark when we found the head of Posey
Holler, and the little church was already surrounded
with men, women, children, and infants in arms, for
it was snake night, when saints and scoffers alike
assembled here. We tied John by a window farthest
from the door, and all ate a buffet supper from the
sill, of cold chicken à la Maryland, and went at once
into the crowded church. The class leader — that
is the leader of the choir — escorted us to the amen
corner by the window outside of which were John
and the cart. Peter whispered that there were signs
of trouble outside, and that in case of a rumpus I
must jump out of the window at once — there might
be fire or a panic inside.

The preacher was young, scarcely more than a
boy, but his face was set in lines too grim for a boy's,
and his large blue eyes burned with a feverish light.
As we rose to sing "What a Friend We Have in
Jesus," members of the class ranged themselves as a
bodyguard before the slender young man and held
their books before their faces; as well they might,
for ripe tomatoes began to whirl through the air. One

struck the wall lamp above me and showered down the glass of the chimney. The class leader calmly replaced the chimney with another, and the class never lost a word of the song, though outside were caterwaulings and pistol shots, and the tomato bombardment continued. But presently the noise ceased as a bent old man with a long gray beard walked slowly up the aisle, bearing a small screened box, inside which I fancied I could see a dark shape writhing. Peter suddenly whispered, "If that petting party comes to this amen corner, it's me for the window!" Fortunately, however, the old man placed the box solemnly before the pulpit, but still all too near us; and I sat with my feet like a Turk's.

Now, one after another, the preacher and the elders prayed long and earnestly for the Power. Over the church resounded the deep voices of the men and the shrill pleadings of the women: "Send the Power! O God, send the Power! Let down the Power!" And when the Power fell upon us was it only fancy that I felt the sweep of wings?

We all rose and shouted, "Glory to God!" And at last the young preacher held out his hand for silence, and read in a low tone the sixteenth chapter of St. Mark. But his voice rang triumphant on the eighteenth verse. "They shall take up serpents; and if they drink any deadly thing, it shall not hurt them; they shall lay hands on the sick, and they shall recover." Softly the class sang, "He walks with me, and He talks with me, and He tells me I am

His own," and the boyish preacher bent over the screened cage and with steady fingers unfastened the top and gently lifted the writhing black form from the box.

Peter whispered hoarsely, "God send the Power holds out!"

The snake made no effort to coil, and, as the boy held it in his open palm, with his right hand over and over again he smoothed the reptile's back. It seemed to me the very church held its breath. "Doped," said Peter. But I knew better, and I whispered a prayer for this young fanatic who offered his life for the faith of another Man, — "if man he can be called," — who died two thousand years ago.

After a while the snake began to try to coil, and slowly and gently the steady hands replaced it in the box. And in the deathlike stillness we distinctly heard that penetrating sound, once heard, never forgotten — the sinister rattle that strikes terror to every living creature. The little church caught its breath. The gnomelike old man bore the screened box down the aisle and out. I prayed that this Christianized snake would live long in captivity. It might be difficult to convert a fresh rattler.

Now the real service began. The preacher preached and the exhorters exhorted, and presently the aisle was filled with groaning, rolling sinners, men, women, and young girls all in an agonized effort "to come through to salvation." Those of us who were not hysterically singing followed the rolling sinners up and down the aisle, murmuring words of comfort, preventing them from injuring each other by unconscious and despairing kicks, and smoothing disarranged apparel. Presently a man leaped to his feet and shouted, "Glory to God! I've come through to salvation!" Then we all shouted, and sang, "I'm Glad Salvation's Free." Now, the ice having been broken, the saved came thick and fast, until there remained but one beautiful young girl, who continued to roll in an agony of unforgiven sin. The woman who sat beside me told me, "That gal has wrastled now fur four nights, and she jest cain't come through nohow. She's the class leader's gal, too." At last the poor girl fell into a kind of trance, and we were compelled to abandon her to her fate for the night.

Outside, for a moment, we huddled together in the chill midnight under the pines. But our tormenters had apparently sought other entertainment after the snake exhibit. The class leader invited us home with him, but we preferred the camp of the Philistines nearer the church. So we told him it was out of our way, and that we wanted to push on before daylight. It was true. We liked to rise while it was yet dark, and to swing through mysterious aisles till the sun rose. Then, while the camp fire burned, I would perhaps catch a fish for breakfast from a near-by stream. This morning we walked slowly, silent, with the spell of the night still upon us. In the eerie dark we heard a soft footfall beside us, and the class leader, whose daughter sought salvation so unsuccessfully, spoke gently from the gloom : —

"I got up airly so 's I could walk a little way with you-all. I wanted to tell you more about our faith."

We sat on a fallen tree under wet muscadine vines; and I have never been able to think of that morning without emotion. The man's theology may have been weak, but the man himself was strong. He had lost everything for his faith : his friends, his position, — he had been a forest ranger, — even his kinsmen, and that, to a mountaineer, is exile. Simple, homely words they were, but weighted with a strange power, a passion that in the dark before the dawn filled his eyes with a chatoyant fire that seemed to light his face. At last he said gently, "We are friends of Jesus, not His servants. He don't trust His servants with secrets. He does trust us. If you-all hain't found Him, jest call. He 'll answer. He come with me this mornin', and He 's here now, like He walked with Cleopas and another man on the way to Emmaus."

We listened in awed silence, but I could not forbear to ask : "But your pure, beautiful young daughter ? Why is it so hard for her to see Him as her friend ?"

He smiled, and I saw his eyes lambent in the dawn — the gentlest eyes I had ever seen.

"Hit 's the purest that sees their sins the blackest. Some little thing holds her back that somebody else would n't notice. But she 'll find Him to-night. I

know hit.   You see, He walks with me this mornin'."
And as he turned away to face the rising sun he
walked with a light step, for did not a Young Man
walk beside him?

"Come," said Peter in the gruff voice which
conceals emotion.   "It 's us for Emmaus and breakfast."

II

ALABAMA, HERE WE REST

WE were resting by the roadside, for it was July and
nearing noon. Even in the cool mountains nature
makes obeisance to the sun at noonday. The singing birds are already hiding in lost green glades, and
the jeweled lizard, forever darting across the white
sand, sleeps now, beneath his broad leaf, as still as
the pebble beside him. After the joyous allegro of
the morning, the crescendo of winds and woods
attains the pause before the languid and prolonged
adagio of a summer afternoon.

We had been walking since sunrise, up and up the
mountain road. Peter, who pushed the cart, was
dejected. He had ivy poison. John, the beloved
mongrel, was dejected. We had taken away his kitten. Two nights before he had brought a scrawny,
badly blondined kitten to camp. He had divided his

corn pone with her, and she slept in the ashes of the camp fire by his side. He insisted that she continue the journey with our party. John, who hates cats! The mystery of the masculine mind! A scrawny little blondined cat! Even we objected to hiking accompanied by a yellow cat; so this morning we presented the kitten to a friendly mountain woman. I am persuaded that John felt it keenly. I too was dejected. I could not forget the little three-year-old boy who plays all day in his old grandfather's blacksmith shop, while his mother lies always sick and alone in the cabin beside it. I could not forget how joyously and competently that curly-haired elf used the tools in the shop where his grandfather's forge had burned for over fifty years, to make his own playthings. The grandfather is very old and the mother cannot last long. There is no one else. What then, for that wonderful little creature? Buddie's father, so the grandfather told me, had kissed him and ridden away into the night.

"Hit war like this," he said. "We-all had allus made good corn whiskey. The sheriff of this county, he owns all the stills now, and he makes whiskey quick with this hyar red-devil lye. Lige, he would n't jine 'em, so one night they come and burned his still, and whooped him and putt him on his horse and driv him outen the country. I could n't holp none. I jest stayed on with Buddie. Whar you-all 'll camp to-night by the big spring is whar the sheriff is buildin' a big pleasure place. But he don't live thar. He lives down in the valley, and he 's got fifty thousand dollars in the bank thar, made outen red-devil lye."

We knew our hike through this particular country held an element of danger. We had been repeatedly warned to turn back, and we had often been stopped by half-drunken men in motor cars and keenly questioned as to our business in these mountains. We had always succeeded in making them believe we were not revenue officers. But we were careful, at night, to set our little tent near a human habitation. We camped that night by the big spring near the sheriff's pleasure place. The caretaker's wife brought us some milk. Milk is buttermilk, in the mountains. Sweet milk is so called and is a luxury. After supper I sat on the porch and talked with the caretaker's wife. A mountain woman talks only of fundamental, basic things of life. She tells me how her husband has pellagra; of her two sons, dead of pellagra. How old am I? And how many children have I? And she tells me if I look away beyond the cotton patch I can see the stone that marks a little grave. "She war my only gal. She choked to death of dipthery. We could n't get no doctor." And I tell her of a little green grave so far away I shall never see it again. We are silent then, but not far apart in spirit, and watch the young moon shine from the lilac west.

The next morning, as we leave, she tells me in her sad monotone, — a mountain woman does not whisper, — very softly, that even Peter may not hear, that I must never leave the pushcart. "Hit won't be safe even with the dog quiled under hit. They 'll putt a bottle of whiskey in hit. Then they 'll catch your man and he 'll have to work out his fine on the road. The convicts air a-buildin' a road fer the automobiles to peddle whiskey on a right smart piece beyant hyar. I reckon I orten to told you. But you-all don't look like you could pay no fine."

Now we were nearing the road the convicts were building. Beyond, on either side we could see the great iron cages — larger, but exactly like the animal cages of the circus — where the convicts lived.

Down the hot road between the iron cages walked a tall, gaunt mountain woman. She was neatly dressed, as are all mountain women outside their homes, and she carried a basket from the crossroads store at the top of the mountain. "Happy Top" it is called. God save the mark!

As the woman reached us, she fixed me with her great fierce eyes and asked, "Air you the woman as is walkin' fer comfort?"

I laughed. I could n't help it. But Peter understood. He knew that *Comfort* is the name of the family paper which has the largest circulation of any paper in America, and that a Pearle someone was writing a hiking experience for this paper. If a mountain woman reads a paper, she reads *Comfort*. I was sorry I was not Pearle. The woman's world

was small. She was disappointed. So I told her I
had a fiddle in the cart, and would she wait, and did
she think I might play for the convicts at noon?

"I 'm scairt they won't want to hear no music
when they belong to eat," she replied. "I reckon
the gyard won't let you nohow. You might play
to-night, after they 're in their cages, ef they all ain't
dead then. Hit 's a powerful hot day fer 'em. Yesterday a little city feller, he fell down a-diggin' in the
sun, and I axed the gyard ef I could n't carry him a
gourd o' water. He would n't let me, and he kicked
the feller up agin and he fell down agin and they
throwed a bucket o' water on to him and let him lay.
He war in a faint. You 'll see him as you pass by.
He wears big specs, and his hands air a-tremblin' so
he can't wipe the sweat off 'n 'em."

"What did he do? What was his crime?" Peter
asks.

"He war a-walkin' down to Gadsden by hisself
and they slipped a bottle o' moonshine in his bundle,
and then ketched him to work out his fine. Thar 's
a ole man — you see him on the left side a-diggin';
hit 's him with the long white whiskers — his wife 's
a-dyin' and he went over on tother mounting to
shoot something — she war a-honin' for something
more 'n hawg meat — and he could n't find nothing
but a chicken a-drinkin' at the crick, and he shot hit
and carried hit home, kind o' brash like — he war
miserble — and they ketched him, and he 's workin'
out his fine, an' the neighbors on tother mounting

air a-holpin' his wife. She's a-dyin' o' pellágra.
The ole man's allus been kind o' lackin'. He's
powerful old, and him bein' lackin' he's kinda off 'n
his haid. He hollers out loud and prays. The
gyards hit him over the haid yesterday when he
hollered to some folks a-passin'. You see the sun is
so hot, an' the ole man's lackin' anyhow."

"There is a store beyond?" I ask faintly. "We
want to buy some alcohol. My husband has ivy
poison."

"Yes," she answered. "Hit's a right smart store.
I don't know about alcohol. The storekeeper he
owns a right smart chance of everything on this and
tother mounting. Sence the boll weevil tuck us we
all owe him duebills, and he owns all the land.
They're about all renters but me. My son's a
engineer in Birmingham. I own my place. He's
a-movin' the mounting to get me out. Good-bye.
I'd be proud if you-all'd write me a card. I kin
read writin' too."

We put John on the chain, and trudged on up
the hot road between the iron cages. Mules and
scrapers; negroes and whites; guards with pistols;
and over all a pall of silence. Dirt and toil and sweat
and torture! The "city feller" with the "specs"
turned away his pallid face; the old man who was
"lackin'" cried out a prayer to us; the guard shook
him roughly by the shoulder. The silent horror of
the road, broken only by the old man's cry, crept
into our blood and caught at our hearts.

The store was packed with silent, lank mountaineers, sitting on boxes, spitting tobacco with great accuracy and perfect regularity from the open windows. Each man took his turn. There was a small amount of denatured alcohol in the lamp. We might have it, but there was no bottle to be found, no can, no receptacle whatever. We were in despair. Peter, tortured with ivy poison, grew more dejected.

A tall, lean mountaineer unfolded himself in sections from his box.

"Stranger," he said, "my advice is to step behind thim flour sacks and putt hit on. Hit 'll be yourn then."

Presently a stifled groan came from behind the flour sacks. The mountaineer spat through the window out of his turn — it was an unusual occasion — and remarked dryly, "All of which he done so."

We camped that night by a stream where I fished. John, barking at every fish I caught, forgot the kitten. Once more he was a gay dog. Peter, the pain of ivy poison allayed, was serene again. Nature healed us. But the old man who was lacking wept in his iron cage for his wife who was dying alone on "tother mounting." God send the pallid city youth slept the sleep of exhaustion. The little boy who played all day by the forge lay beside his tubercular mother in the cabin near the shop. Perhaps the father who would n't join the sheriff in making red-

devil whiskey thinks of them to-night. The caretaker's wife, whose husband has pellagra, rocks in
the moonlight that shines on the grave of a child
"that thar war n't no doctor to holp."

O America! Land of peace and plenty. Alabama! Here we rest.

III

THE SACRED HARP SING

In a remote glen of the green little mountains of Alabama, the wheel of Sisyphus broke.

We were on our way, this day, to the Sacred Harp Sing, and we had six miles of lonely mountain road, bordered on either side by hidden illicit stills, before we came to camp at Hard Shell Churchyard. We could not abandon Sisy. Our summer home was there with Sis: our tent, our blankets, our violin, kodak, and cooking outfit. John suggested the way out. He simply trotted on, hopefully. So did we. And there a little way on, under a great oak, lay Endymion, asleep in full noontide. Endymion, with the high, broad forehead of the mountaineer, the brown curls, the firm mouth, and the straight nose. Ah, the blessed straight noses of these mountain people! We make our mouths; our eyes are the windows of the soul — dimmed maybe, and with a light out or broken; but our noses are a kind of landed estate we carry about with us. They proclaim our ancestry, and no amount of acquired culture can change them. Endymion sat up, and in a somewhat dazed but courtly manner asked us the same question we had been answering for two days: "Air you-all on your way to the Sacred Harp Sing?"

With his assistance we patched the wheel of Sisyphus, and by sunset were in camp at the Hard Shell Churchyard. Quick or dead, I have a penchant for sleeping in a country churchyard. When the shadows creep down from the mountains, and pallid mists writhe and wreathe above their mysterious summits, there is a certain comfort in the spires man has lifted from, perhaps, his primitive awe of mountain and mist.

The next morning we pushed Sisyphus, called John, and found ourselves in the country-seat town, completely surrounded by mules. There were mules ridden, and mules driven to every conceivable vehicle. As the mountaineer says, "Nary a horse." Though, later, hundreds of motor cars glided in. And such a well-behaved, well-dressed Sabbath gathering! Such clean, stalwart youths, and such delicately beautiful women! Even from hickory chairs of rickety wagons there descended, always, tasteful and modish costumes.

The Sacred Harp Sing convened at the pretentious stone courthouse. Alabama courthouses are invariably all glorious without and all dilapidated within. The room on the second floor was packed with fifteen hundred souls. The high ceilings were discolored, and the walls were peeling. Spittoons by the dozen failed to protect the floor. A patriarch, with a beautiful Websterian head, occupied the judge's stand. His long chin worked continuously for exactly seven hours — eight, if we include the dinner hour. I thought it was palsy, but was told it was "jes' chawin' terbaccer."

Fifty men, women, and children sat about the jury box. This was the "class." We opened the Sing with a few words of prayer, then the President of the Sacred Harp Sing advanced and waved a long, bony hand. Around the class he gave the signal — sol, fay, la. It was repeated solemnly by the class, and suddenly we all burst into such a sol-fay-la-ing that literally the ears ached.

A silence — then the leader rolled his eyes heavenward and reverently announced the "words." We were never permitted the words until we had sol-fay-ed the melody. We sang continuously for seven hours, with one hour's intermission for the "spread dinner." We sang everything from an exhilarating one-step of "Amazing Grace" to the gentle fox trot of "Don't Grieve Your Mother, Don't Grieve Your Ma," which called for the only encore. Leaders were changed every fifteen minutes, and often beautiful

little girls were lifted to the table and waved their
tiny hands about the class for the sol-fay-ing of the
first rendition.

The President informed me that a dispute raged
between the followers of the "Sacred Harp" book
and another called, I think, "Christian Harmony."
The bone of contention was alto. The President
himself did not hold with alto. But, as six counties
were represented at this Sing, he was for compromise,
and used both books. He told me that in a Sacred
Harp Sing only four notes were permitted — mi, fay,
sol, la; and that the four-note system originated at
Pentecost, where the Disciples just naturally burst
into song; and that for his part he did not believe
there was an alto present.

"Of course," he said, "these songs were sung first
at our own firesides, then in the deestrict schools.
Hit was in the deestrict schools," he said sadly,
"that the alto crept in. Now we sing everywhar,
county conventions and state conventions. Say a
good word for us, sister. Ours is a work of sanctifica-
tion. We mean to sanctify the world by song."

That night, as I lay in our little tent, I said,
"Peter, what is it all about? This sacred jazz of
four holy notes, and a compromise on heretical alto?
Is it a dawning musical consciousness? Is it an
expression of religious emotion — a kind of Indian
Corn dance? Is it simply the conservative South
preserving her memories?"

"Not so conservative," said Peter. "This is one

of the four Republican counties of Alabama. It is their annual Passion Play."

"Was it really religious emotion? Those leaders were as vain as peacocks."

"Oh, as to that," said Peter, "it 's all the same thing — sex expression. But one thing — it is sincere. There is no graft. The President has no salary. He is a poor farmer raising cotton for the landlord and the boll weevil."

"There 's my good word for the President!" I cry, and turn to sleep contentedly.

And yet, six counties of well-dressed, sophisticated people — even sordid Birmingham, where thousands walk the streets unemployed, was represented — all sol-fay-ing for seven mortal hours to sanctify an agonized world.

"Where but in America?"

IV

MOUNTAINEERS AND MILL FOLKS

WE camped beside the blanched road near the foot
of the hill, where we could lie and look across the
shining ford of the little river into the moon-drenched
valley below. The mountaineer in the near-by cabin
had said, "Ef you-all won't sleep hyar, you 'd best
go on half a quarter and sleep in the schoolhouse.
The mill folks carries liquor down this road sometimes. They goes up tother way, but sometimes
they comes back by hyar — hit 's a lonesomer way.
And you best tie up you-all's dog. The mill folks
jist runs over our houn's lickety-split! They won't
mis-putt theyselves ter stop whin they kills one
even."

But vacant schoolhouses were not for us. For
there we heard sounds of revelry by night, and the

smell of liquor lingered there by day, and the floors
were often deep in dirt and torn textbooks. Once
during a drizzling rain we had camped for three days
in a schoolhouse where four men kept their tools,
which they said were for digging graphite — though
we saw no evidence of graphite and much evidence
of moonshine. One of these men asked us for our
newspapers received at the last mountain post office.

"I 'm the onliest one thet kin read in this settlemint, and whin I gits a-holt of a paper I reads hit to
all the neighbors. I cain't read writin', though. I
wusht I could," he ended wistfully. Peter asked
him if he could not learn to write at the school here.
He answered, "This hyar schoolhouse hes ben built
three yars, and thar hain't ben a term o' school in
hit. Whut with the boll weevil and the chillern
hevin' ter work and all the likely young folks gone
down ter the mill, thar hain't nobody ter go noways."

But this night there was a full moon, and witchery
was in the air. For months we had slept under the
stars, seldom putting up our little tent, though
always carefully packing Sisyphus in case of a storm
or a sudden alarm. A night under the open sky is a
royal adventure; and sleep under a full moon is not
an abdication. For sleep means not merely surcease
from sorrow while the "sleave of care" is knitted;
the full moon is a silver trumpet calling a challenge
from some enchanted world of otherwhereness, which
we answer bravely, taking consciousness gladly to
new fields of magic where the moon is a monarch.

Earth, under the full moon, answers the call with a quickened pulse, and the water's lagging feet obey her lyric summons with a quickened measure. Even John gazed at the moon and howled mournfully from the depths of some dread memory in answer to her solemn call. But when a mocking bird, teetering on the very tip of a dogwood bough above him, — a premeditated insult, — burst into a passion of song, John, chained to the wheel of Sisyphus, stiffened in resentment, turned around four times, flung himself to earth, and slept. And after a while there was whispering in the willows by the river, and a little breeze, drugged with the scent of honeysuckle, stole out and softly touched our faces — and we too slept.

In the chill of the night we were awakened by the noise of a motor car clattering down the mountain road. It splashed through the ford and groaned a sudden stop, and a woman's drunken laugh profaned the night. John leaped the length of his chain as two men ran from the car and stood upon our blankets. I looked up into the face of one, who grasped my arm and cried, "Get up and come on down to the schoolhouse!" But Peter had seized the loaded rifle by his side and, pointing it at the man's head, said icily, in his best chest tones, "Gentlemen, we are sleeping here by permission of the landowner; and we do not desire to be disturbed." With the rifle waving before them they backed silently to the car, and presently from the schoolhouse came sounds of drunken revelry.

"Here," I said, "is where I take up my bed and walk. They will come back, and we shall be compelled to shoot someone." And not long after we heard yells and shots at our abandoned camp.

The next morning the mountain woman said, "Hit wuz some o' thim mill folks. I knows who hit wuz. They hain't bad folks. They wuz drinkin' and they 'll be pow'ful 'shamed this mornin'. They ust ter live up hyar. But 'pears like whin they gits down ter the mill they jist goes hawg-wild! You know," she went on, fixing her great melancholy eyes on the far horizon of the mountains, "they 's ben lonesome so long."

"Ya-a-s," said the man, "my womern 's got kin down ter the mill, and oncet she went thar ter visit 'em. I had a great chancet o' peaches thet yar, and hit did n't dis-abundance me ter send some, and hit did n't mis-putt Viney ter take 'em. Viney says they did n't can up a one! They jist sets down and et 'em up and give 'em away. They even don't bake they own bread. Jist runs out and buys a loaf, — they 's a big store they calls a commissary, — and eats and lights out fur thim picture movies. Hit seems ter make 'em go hawg-wild ter git ter the mill. They forgits Gawddlemighty *en*-tire!"

We set out on the road to the mill with reluctance. But at the mill was the only bridge across the river to Deer Mountain, where we wished to go. So we loitered on the way, and in the afternoon there suddenly appeared on the summit of the mountain, overlooking the valley of the mill, a place that simply demanded a camp. Back from a grassy meadow sprawled an old unpainted house under immense pine trees. At the right was a cuplike dell filled with blossoming altheas. Everywhere we had found altheas in door-yards; for an althea twig makes the best snuff stick, and a snuff stick is a salient feature of a mountain woman's face. But these altheas were almost trees, and trembling above and among the blossoms were hundreds of humming birds, the Western sun glinting their tiny green feathers until they shimmered with myriad iridescent hues.

We went through the big gate, and I could scarcely get Peter, John, and Sisyphus past the fascinating open workshop at the left. From the house came a woman in a long brown calico dress. She was so tall and so thin that, as she came rapidly across the grass, she seemed to be walking on stilts. And her great black eyes, glassy with age, burned with unquenched fire as she cried, "Ef you-all air sellin' medicine, you-all need n't come in! I sells all the medicine this hyar mounting needs. I ben arrested fur hit. But I jist tole 'em ter crack they whup! I jist go on sellin'. 'T ain't no ust comin' in hyar!"

We explained meekly that we were only attracted by the beauty of the place, and wanted to camp for the night by the humming birds in the dell. Around the corner of the house, walking softly on the myrtle, solid and thick as a carpet, a small clean-shaven old man drifted toward us. We afterward found that he never approached a destination other than obliquely. John ran forward to meet him and stood statuelike in amazement. For the man had a Captain Cuttle hook for his left hand, only this was of two iron prongs tied to his wrist by a leather thong.

"James," said the woman, "these hyar folks thinks our place is so purty they wants ter stay all night."

"Hit is a purty place," said the old man gently. "Hit ust ter be a great place fur the highrostocracy afore the war atween the States. They ust ter come frum the South with they niggers and they carriages. They 's a fine chalybeate spring jist past thim posies down the hill. The chimbleys is thar yit whar they burnt the big hotels in the war. Come round ter the back door and see whar they ust ter dance. Thar 's names cyarved on the rock frum way back."

Worn smooth by the dancing feet of forgotten belles and beaus lay an enormous rock, level as a floor, on the edge of a precipice overlooking a wide valley. An old insecure iron fence protected one who dared look down.

"Be keerful!" warned the old man. "Ef we hed iny chillern I 'd fix thet fence." I looked eagerly at the names carved there, and exclaimed when I found one I knew. The date was 1824.

"Yas," said the man, "my grandpappy knowed thim folks. I ricollect hit, fur the name wuz so quare."

"De la Vergne," I said.

"Thet 's hit!" he cried. "They all kim frum the North, and one of 'em painted a picter o' whar my grandpappy's pigpen war. And hit 's framed and hangin' in our house hyar. And one like hit sold fur money. And one time my granny said thet Mr. Devilin et at her house, and she hed ter rub his plate with a onion, though he would n't eat no onion. I 've heerd her tell hit and laugh!"

"That was my great-grandfather," I said.

"Think o' thet, Marthy! Ole Mr. Devilin 's her great-grandpappy! Come right in the house 'n' rest! Er maybe you-all 'd like ter try some o' my seedlin' peaches? I keeps the finest tree fur my friends. Thar 's four props under hit this yar. I never sells a peach frum hit. I calls hit my Friends' Tree."

"Humph!" said his wife acidly. "They is all his friends' trees! He won't sell nothin' fur whut hit 's wuth!"

"Now, Marthy," he answered patiently, "I sells 'em. But to sell too expensive is whut the Bible calls 'doublin' and thriblin',' and hit 's agin the Book."

"Oh, thet Bouk! Thet Bouk!" she cried contemptuously. "I 'll bring out some cheers and knives, and you-all jist set under the tree and eat. Thet 's whut all his friends does!"

"Don't mind Marthy. Marthy 's a good Christian womern, though she don't seem to reelize hit. See this hat? Hit 's a good hat," he said, removing his wide gray felt. "I hain't hed hit but two yars

and hit 's all frayed on the aidge. You see, mornin's
after chorin 's done I th'ows hit in the kitchen door,
and ef hit comes rollin' back I lights out fur the work
shed and waits around a spell. But ef hit don't
come bouncin' back, I jist walks right in ter breakfast."

The Friends' Tree, near the house, stood on a little
knoll overlooking the valley, and under the four
props was a bower where one could sit and, without
rising, pick the rosy peaches. Our host said, "Don't
take iny but the very finest. Thar 's more 'n we 'll
eat. I hain't got enough friends! Whin you-all
eats all you want, come round ter the back porch.
They 's some sugar-sweet mushmelons I ben wantin'
somebody ter try."

It was an experience to see the old man wash his
iron hand, deftly carve a melon, and offer a slice
politely on a prong. John turned surprised and
delighted eyes on me, as if to say, "Here is a man
that is a man!"

"Whut 's you-all's name?" called the woman from
the kitchen door. We told her, and she said, "Our
name 's Brent, but iverbody calls us Aunt Marthy
and Uncle James. I reckon you-all kin too.
Why n't you-all come in the house? I don't like
folks ter light on me and stay in the yard!"

"I 'll go round and roll you-all's little wagon inter
a room," said Uncle James.

We explained that for our health we preferred to
camp outdoors. Aunt Marthy sniffed something

about "pink pills fur pale people," and we entered the great beamed kitchen with its huge fireplace and polished stove. At the east was an open door with a fence across it, which looked down a sheer drop of hundreds of feet. And as Aunt Marthy bent her tall form and vehemently threw out the dishwater I trembled for fear she would bring up in the valley below.

It rained for the next two days, and we moved into the house, which leaked like a sieve.

"Git yerself cheers and hunt a dry spot and set down," said Aunt Marthy, who was occupying the most commodious spot, engaged in quilting a wonderful Texas Star quilt. "James wants ter putt on a new roof. But we're old, and we hain't much comp'ny, and thar's allers spots fur cheers whar hit don't leak — though we cain't allers set in the same room, the leaks not bein' in the right spots. Kin you-all read print?"

Peter answered that we could.

"Wal, I got a book. Hit's titled *Leny Rivers*, by Mary J. Holmes. I've hed hit more'n twinty yars, and whiniver inybody comes as kin read they reads hit ter me. I cain't read, and James won't read nothin' but newspaper lies and thet Bouk! Lord, I've hed ter hyar so much about thet Bouk thet hit's plumb spiled my natur'! I don't hold with cussin', but iver' time James says 'the Bouk' I feel like tellin' him who died fur him!"

And Aunt Marthy opened a trunk and carefully

unwrapped *Lena Rivers* from a blue silk handkerchief.

The pride of a mountain woman's heart is a trunk. Though she has never traveled, nor ever expects to travel, and would be aghast at the thought, her social position is determined by the size and quality of her trunk; and Aunt Marthy smiled appreciatively when Peter cried, "Some trunk!"

So I followed Lena from childhood in the country to adolescence in the cruel city, when suddenly Aunt Marthy called to Peter, who sat with Uncle James in respective dry spots in the next room.

"Hyar you, Peter! You read a spell. She's tired."

"Aunt Marthy," said Peter mendaciously, "I've read — er — *Lena* — er — *Riverton.* I'll read you a good piece out of my paper."

"In case o' thet," said Uncle James, "I'll bring my harness in ter mend. I've hed ter hyar *Leny* in spots fur more 'n twinty yars — though I cain't say I 've iver connected hit up."

Peter hurriedly selected a back-to-the-land article. With fervor it called the weary wayworn city dweller back to the farm, and urged him to relax, relax. Aunt Marthy looked bored. She took snuff, spat, missed, and looked mortified. She said, "Fur Gawd's sake, Peter, whut is that air ree-lax and how do you do hit?"

Peter gave me an appealing glance, and I said, "He means 'to ease up — not try too hard. Be peaceful.' He wants the poor tired city man to go on a farm and — er — relax, you know."

"Humph!" cried Aunt Marthy, and missed the fireplace again. "Thet man 's got a farm ter sell! Does he think we gits a ree-lax outen hoein' cawn and choppin' cotton, er raisin' leetle things like chickens and calves jist ter kill 'em er sell 'em ? The onliest ree-lax I kin git on a farm is ter kill a rattler in my sang patch, er look down the bar'l o' my gun at a revenue officer! Now, Peter — you jist quit that ree-lax piece and read some in *Leny*."

Peter, anxious to avoid *Leny* and to cover his lack of literary taste, said, "I looked down the barrel of my rifle on the road last night." I told the story, and Aunt Marthy cried, "Hit wuz thim no-count ornery mill folks! I wusht you-all 'd shot 'em whilst you-all hed the chancet!"

"Now, now, Marthy," said Uncle James, "they is jist the same folks thet ust ter be our friends — least-ways they mammies and pappies wuz. I don't 'low they would a harmed you-all. But whin they gits ter the mill, civileyezation takes holt and hit ruinates thim fur a while — jist like a fever takes holt. They is ust ter still places, and Gawddlemighty, and lonesomeness, and they don't know how ter be in the world and out of hit too like the Good Book tells us ter be. You never knows whut civileyezation 's a-goin' ter do whin hit fust takes holt. Now you take Willie Lemon — he 's jist Hell-bent fur civileyezation. You see, thar is Willie Lemon —"

"Ya-a-a-s," said Aunt Marthy cynically, "thar *is* Willie Lemon! I see him stanterin' th'ough the huckleberry patch now, comin' down the mounting ter set under yo' Friends' Tree and hyar you norate! Willie Lemon ort ter be shot fur laziness. He don't work a lick!"

"Willie hain't ter say lazy exactly. He claims he's diskivered hit hain't no use ter work, and the Book does say ter take no thought fur the morrer."

Peter, intrigued by this fascinating doctrine, asked, "Who is Willie Lemon?" Aunt Marthy answered gladly, "Willie Lemon's a woods colt. His mammy war Lily Ann Lemon, and I wuz thar whin he wuz borned. She war a-layin' thar white as death and iverbody thought a-dyin', and the preacher he come and told Lily Ann she'd go to Hell ef she did n't tell who the pappy wuz and confess her sin; and she jist smiled and niver said a word, and got well and met a mill feller and married him and left Willie with his grandpappy and he died too. And Willie he ketches rattlers and sells the ile and the skins th'ough the mail order. He won't trap, fur he won't kill nothin' but a rattler er a copperhead. I claim Willie Lemon is lackin', myself."

"No, Willie hain't lackin'. But he war a quare young un. He war four yar old afore he'd speak a word. One day they kotched a big rat, and they war a-showin' hit in a trap, and they all went outen the room, and whin they comes back the rat wuz gone, and they wuz a-marvelin', and Willie Lemon up and says, 'I let that rat out, and I 'm glad I done hit!' Fust word he iver spoke! And whin he went ter school he jist set thar, and the teacher, thinkin' he wuz lackin', jist let him set. And one day whin thar wuz a sum a big boy could n't do, Willie went ter the blackboard and done the sum right, and set down and never said a word. No, Willie hain't lackin'."

"Hyar he comes th'ough the big gate," said Aunt Marthy.

But Willie Lemon did not come through the big gate. He came over it like a bird, and with one continuous gesture he cart-wheeled across the grass with a bunch of white grapes in his hand, which he presented to Aunt Marthy, apparently without the loss of a grape. And Willie Lemon was the most perfect specimen of the human race we had ever seen. He was twenty-three, of medium height, broad of shoulder and small of thigh. His jet-black hair might have been permanently waved at a beauty parlor; his skin was milk-white and apparently did not tan. For, unlike the mountaineer, he wore no hat. His features were like chiseled marble, and his soft black eyes under their curling lashes gleamed with veiled fire beneath their gentleness. During the week we spent with Aunt Marthy he came every day, and he never spoke but to answer a question, though he was quick to see when any helpful act could be performed for any of us.

Willie Lemon seemed closer to his hands, his feet,

his head, his body, than other human creature ever was. I spoke of this one day, and Uncle James said, "Willie, show how you kin walk on yer haid." Obligingly Willie bounced away over the grass on his head, gracefully and seemingly without effort. We used to speculate as to whether Willie Lemon *was* his body, or whether he stood outside his body and commanded it. And one day, as we all sat on the gallery, Willie Lemon, as ever silent, and with his eyes fixed on the distant mountains, suddenly arose and ran off in a direction opposite from his home.

"Willie's had a call," said Aunt Marthy.

"Yes, he has 'em too, like Samuel in the Good Book, and like —"

"Shucks!" cried Aunt Marthy. "I reckon Samuel did n't smell a rattler whin he had a call! I claim he smells 'em! I 'low Willie Lemon kin smell a rattler miles away!"

And after a while Willie returned, carrying a huge rattlesnake, with twelve rattles, on a stick.

"Whar 'd ye find hit, Willie?" asked Uncle James admiringly.

"Hit war a mile down the road under the stile whar the Reed chillern passes frum school. I jist got thar afore 'em."

The day before we left he suddenly spoke to me. "Do you-all know inybody in Kansas City?" he asked.

I told him I once lived there.

"I wusht I knowed someone thar. I larned about

automobiles by mail order frum thar, all about 'em
and how ter drive one. I 'm a-goin' thar."

"Oh, Willie Lemon!" I answered, pained.
"Why? Why?"

"I wants ter putt my hand on er wheel and go
faster 'n iny varmint in these hyar mountings.
Sometime I wants er airship."

So that was why Uncle James knew that "civileyezation had tuck holt o' Willie Lemon"!

We gave him a letter to someone we knew in
Kansas City, and I doubt not that Willie Lemon
stood silent for a time before some garage or factory,
and suddenly proved his ability to drive in a race!

There came a day when for the last time I took the
perilous path down through the altheas to the chalybeate spring by the desolate chimneys of the old
hotels. And as I climbed back up the rocky way I
wondered how those delicate women of America's
feudalism, in their hoop skirts and thin slippers, ever
managed to reach the dancing rock. I walked for
the last time through the grove of altheas, where the
humming birds, not at all afraid of me, bobbed about
like tiny soap bubbles iridescent in the sunlight; and
I walked across the thick, soundless myrtle and sat
down on the edge of the gallery to rest. Through
the open window came the voice of Uncle James in
melancholy groans.

"I tole you, James Brent," cried Aunt Marthy's
voice, "I tole you whut 'd happen ef you et so many
o' thim mushmelons! Now jist groan away!"

"Hit hain't thet, Marthy! Hit hain't mushmelons! Hit's Peter and Eleanor!" He groaned
again. "They is good folks! Fine folks! But
they lives down thar in civileyezation, and they
hain't obeyed they Book's commands. Good folks!
Fine folks! And lost! Lost!"

And he groaned again.

Aunt Marthy hissed one famous Napoleonic word
which expressed all her contempt for creeds outworn;
and I tiptoed across the myrtle to the Friends' Tree,
hardly knowing whether to laugh or to weep.

Peter sat under the tree, and as I saw Uncle James
emerge from the house, followed by his hat, and tack
toward the workshop, I knew he would come to
anchor presently at the peach tree. So I said,
"Here comes Uncle James to speak to us about our
souls. Be careful not to hurt him. He is suffering
about our souls."

"Our souls!" cried Peter in a frightened voice,
slipping the Little Blue Book of Nietzsche into his
pocket.

Uncle James took off his hat, and spoke with grave
dignity. "I don't aim ter be brash ner conceitful,
but I feels I jist gotter speak ter you afore you-all
leaves. I knows hit's hard ter keep onspotted frum
the world, down in civileyezation whar you-all
belongs ter go back ter. And now Willie Lemon,
he's Hell-bent fur hit too — and I jist cain't stand
hit, somehow! I've watched civileyezation take holt
o' our own mounting folks down at the mill and —"

He turned away his head and wiped his eyes with his red handkerchief.

Peter, nervous about his soul and anxious to confuse the issue, said, "But, Uncle James, civilization is just an easier way of doing things. Just machinery. Now those mill folks, their natural needs — things they have always wanted — are for the first time being supplied. It 's like food to a starving man. It intoxicates them — makes them hysterical —"

"Peter," said Uncle James, gently but reproachfully, "hit hain't as ef I could n't read. I kin read the plain commands o' the Good Book, and I takes the *Atlanty Constitution*, and I knows about civileyezation. Thet thar machinery jist kills thousands and thousands jist runnin' over folks, and in mines and factories. And the folks as owns 'em is doublin' and thriblin' and makin' some folks rich and some folks pore, and nobody keers! I wuz in civileyezation a whole yar oncet, and I lef' my hand thar twell the Resurrection, whin please Gawd I 'll hev hit agin! Fur the Lord is comin' in His power sooner 'n you know! And — and — I reckon you-all hain't even ever ben baptized!"

"Uncle James," I cried desperately, "whatever God you love, I 'm sure I love Him too!"

"Hit hain't enough, honey," he said, patting my arm with his iron prongs, "we gotter obey thim plain commands."

Blessed Aunt Marthy called at this moment, —

for I should have committed myself to anything, —
"You-all quit listenin' ter James and come in ter
dinner. This is you-all's last day and you-all gotter
eat with me. I got fried chicken and chess pie!"

Uncle James smiled in a relieved way, and placed
his peace barometer firmly on his head. Peter, in
the freemasonry of men, cried, "Fair weather, and
mild, Uncle James"

"Yes," he said. "Now you take Marthy. Once
saved, allers saved. Marthy's saved, though she
don't know hit. But you see, she's obeyed thim
commands — and I'm afeared you-all hain't."

"Uncle James," said Peter, "those commands
have made a mighty good man out of you. And I
promise to read them all over again." And we did.

The next morning, as we looked back at the old
house under the pines, and at the althea dell, and at
Aunt Marthy and Uncle James waving from the big
gate, I brushed the tears from my eyes and said,
"Maybe we'll meet them again under the Friends'
Tree in Paradise. But it will not be the same.
Aunt Marthy's dear wicked fire will be quenched,
and Uncle James will walk directly on those golden
streets, and he'll not have the Captain Cuttle hand,
and he will have lost that lovely blend of wisdom
and superstition!"

"But," said Peter, "if Uncle James wants to gain
his hand and lose his naïveté we shouldn't stand in
his way!"

"Therein," I answered, "is a mystery. The

problem of love, and growth, and separation and everything. We'll consider that at the camp fire to-night."

But there was no camp fire that night or for several nights. For, arriving at the valley of the mill, civilization "tuck holt," and we moved into a large vacant hotel where from our deep window ledge we could drop a penny — and I did — into the chuckling water of the river below. Across the road, in the great red brick mansion with its white stone pillars and spacious grounds, lived a delightful family, and there was music in the evenings, and much talk of books. For they were lonely folks, burdened with household cares; and, while the mill continued to run, no one could be persuaded to go out to service.

Peter spent much of his time at the woolen mill. But, after once seeing that the piteous bundles of fleeces — shipped in from some place where civilization had "tuck strong holt" — were filled with rags, old iron, and old shoes to increase the weight, I wandered, instead, among the shabby, neglected homes of the mill people, where no blooming geraniums in tin cans adorned the windows, as in all mountain homes. For the home is kept by a child too young to work at the mill, or a woman too old.

One morning I stopped at a shackly house where an old woman sat with a child on the little porch. Observing that the boy did not run about, I asked if he were sick. "No," she answered, "he's jist got the rickets. We hes a heap o' lung trouble and rickets hyar. But lawsy, whin we had pellagry up in the mountings we jist up and died without no doctor. We got good doctors hyar."

"But don't you sometimes wish for the mountains?" I asked.

"Me? I would n't go back to thim mountings fur nothin' in this hyar world! Allers choppin' cotton, and splittin' stove wood, and niver seein' nobody! We-uns is goin' ter hev a dance 'cross the river frum the hotel ternight. You-all come over."

I thanked her and told her we would, and that they were decorating the hotel also for a dance to-night, and many of the guests and the music would come from the state capital. I asked her if she would like to come and watch the dance with us.

"No 'm, I don't 'low as I will. I don't keer fur thet bellerin' music. I 've heerd hit. Some o' our mill girls 'd like ter dance like thim city folks, but our men won't dance with 'em like thet. You cain't git 'em ter jiggle round and kick out behint like thet! Cain't even git our manager ter dance like thet, but he goes to 'em — reckon he jist has ter caper to thim city folks."

That night the guests arrived in cars and danced to an excellent jazz band. By the window where we sat two old men, mill hands, looked on from outside. The floor manager approached them and said civilly, "Move on, will you? We need the air. The ladies complain that it is too warm."

One of the men replied easily, "Wal, I would n't 'low as they needs more air. They don't 'per ter hev on no more clo'es than 'd wad a shotgun." And they walked quietly away.

We followed them across the bridge to the mill dance. A solitary fiddler sat in the fork of a tree, playing "Money Musk." Children danced together on the grass, and the grandmother of the child with the rickets swung about the small platform and "balanced all" with the best of them. I dare say that moonshine as well as moonlight contributed to the joy of the occasion, but there was no rowdyism, and no hint of envy of the hotel dance across the river. For these mill folks are mountaineers or descendants of mountaineers, proud of their heritage and tenacious of their customs. So they danced the summer night happily away, forgetting the day's toil and the threat of to-morrow's drudgery — for they were together.

V

A GEORGIA PEACH

THE Belles of Georgia were *passées*. But there still remained those too ripe for shipment. And if you have never eaten a rejected Belle of Georgia in the orchard, you have never eaten a peach! But we saw that they were picking the Elbertas; so we pushed Sisyphus up the mountain, and stopped before the caretaker's cabin to ask for work. Not that we especially desired work; but we desired peaches in such quantity, and for so long a period, that work seemed the best way to acquire them.

The caretaker's dog, disregarding our beloved mongrel's pathetic friendliness, and utterly ignoring the usual sign of amity, growled an insulting remark about our appearance, which John resented. The pickers were passing from their day's work, and we were at once divided into conscientious objectors and jingoes. Peter seized John by the tail, the caretaker seized his dog in a like manner, and there was an enforced armistice. It seemed an inauspicious moment in which to ask for work, but we did. The mountaineer grinned, and said: "The fo'eman, he 's gone ter town, but you-all kin move inter the shack next mine, and I reckon he 'll take you-all on in the mornin'. Ever pick er pack?"

Peter replied that we were experienced, as indeed we are. For Peter has experienced the orange industry, and I have paid off several installments of my karma owning and operating alone a large commercial apple orchard wished on me in the Middle West.

So we borrowed a broom, put John on his chain, and pushed Sis into the cabin, where in the rock fireplace the kettle boiled cheerfully before nightfall.

The next morning at sunrise we climbed the steep rocky path to the packing shed. The great, clean, open pavilion sat on the very pinnacle of the mountain, overlooking one hundred acres of peach trees *en talus*, each rocky terrace just wide enough for a footing below its row of trees. On every side the sun glinted on blue billows of distant mountains, their summits gleaming with rainbow mists forever dissolving in the serene air. Spring comes late up this way, and in a few short weeks works, with tremendous fervor, her creative will. And early the drowsy earth croons her summer song of enchantment and tranced calm. We sat before a packing table, and

in the brooding quiet listened expectantly for the
pipe of a shepherd on a hillside.

Suddenly Peter glared at me with an anxious eye.
"Those Elbertas!" he cried. "They are not colored.
They are picking too green!" And he hurried down
to inspect the fruit. I was not moved to vicarious
anxiety, and remained to reflect that after all these
weeks of idle wandering along the open road, like
happy gypsies of an older day, we had deliberately
turned aside into this disquieting avenue of trade.

Peter returned with his worst fears confirmed.
But I gently reminded him that this orchard was not
ours, and invited him to watch the workers who were
assembling. For there entered a *grande dame* with a
regal air, followed by other grandes dames equally
queenly. A bevy of girls in gowns of blue, and gold,
and pink, and lavender, with little aprons daintily
embroidered, flitted in like butterflys, followed by
slim youths in clean blouses, with old-fashioned faces
like Civil War daguerreotypes. The grandes dames
sat in comfortable corners and opened books or
magazines. Someone played a fox trot on a har-
monica, and presently the young people were dancing. They danced happily, with grace and decorum,
and it was a sweet sight in the summer morning.

"No poor whites here," said Peter. "These are
the old-time aristocrats, eaten out by the boll weevil.
I'm glad I'm not the fo'eman!"

The foreman appeared. He was a plump, blonde,
pompous young man, and I fancied these people

called him a Yankee. For at once the dancing stopped, and an air almost of sullenness settled upon us. Peter was hired as a picker, but I hesitated and did not apply, though I am rather an expert packer. But without, under the trees, there were too many conferences, with some show of unpleasantness, between the owner and the buyer, and the foreman seemed irritated and confused. At noon Peter told me he had at once discovered the trouble. The brown rot had suddenly developed, and the owner was forcing green peaches on the buyer, in the hope of saving his crop. The poor foreman was at his wit's end, attempting to teach these experienced pickers to pick green, and to force the packers to make a dishonest pack. His attempts at pleasantry, in his crisp Northern voice, were met with respectful silence, and his sharp reprimands with quiet scorn.

I sat near the foreman's desk, and heard him say to a youth who arrived late, "We're picking as green as we can to-day," and he gave him a sample peach to carry. It was very green indeed. When this particular youth returned with his basket, the buyer happened in, and both he and the foreman stepped quickly to examine the fruit. Before the buyer could speak, the foreman cried, "What do you mean by picking green peaches! Ain't you got no sense? Take these out to the culls!" The young man produced his sample peach. "Your own sample that you gave me to pick by," he said. "It's no such thing!" yelled the foreman. "What are you talking about?" and he seized the peach and threw it outside.

The youth's face turned as white as death, and every woman stopped packing. But he said in a controlled voice, "My time, if you please."

"You bet you can have your time, and anybody else can that don't pick honest!" And the foreman went to his desk, where he was a long time making out the check, for every packer arose and walked to the trembling youth.

"Aunt Louise," he said firmly, "take the girls and go back to work. You too, Cousin Carrie — all of you. This is my affair. Just business, you know." He accepted his check with a bow, and the foreman scrawled on the signboard : —

I am the foreman of this orchard and no back talk aloud — Harry Watson.

The pickers filed by the sign with lowered eyes; only Peter laughed.

That evening, in the village, a young man challenged the foreman to fight. He refused, and was gently spanked before an admiring audience. (No doubt Uncle Jeff or Cousin Lee remitted the fine; for all these people seem related.) The next day there was another foreman. No doubt the Northern foreman returned with vivid tales of the lawless South. The new foreman was a Southerner, less efficient, but with the leisurely executive ability that somehow gets things done. The Southerner knows what to slight — and the one to slight!

Still, with every truckload starting to the railway, there was bickering between the owner and the buyer. I was sorry for the owner, who stood to lose his crop. And, after all, a peach is considered ripe when it splits from the seed, and these did. But flavor comes with color on the tree. The orange grower openly gases his fruit for color, and the apple orchardist trusts the apples to color in the box or barrel. They may. But the consumer misses the delicate flavor.

VI

PREACHERS

SATURDAY evening I said, "Let's get out the map and find a county with no railway. 'The world is too much with us.'"

"Yes," said Peter, spreading our tattered map on the floor, "'getting and spending, we lay waste our powers.'"

We found the county, and decided to follow the first beckoning road that led south. Then I rose happily, and deliberately swallowed three tablets of permanganate of potash, mistaking John's mange wash for charcoal tablets. By the time an emetic was prepared, my throat was too constricted for relief, and the caretaker rushed us in his Ford to the village physician.

The doctor sat on his porch, smoking his evening pipe. The caretaker called, "Hi, Doc! Hyar's a

orchard womern jist swallered pizen." Peter cried,
"Permanganate of potash!" The doctor, without
removing his pipe, waved a patronizing hand and
drawled, "Drive on to the drug store; he 'll know the
antidote."

The druggist reached for a dusty tome and began
to read. After a reasonable time Peter reminded
him that there was a woman present who was
poisoned, and that it seemed a poor time for reading.
He continued his search, but Peter called the doctor
over the telephone. The doctor said that he did n't
remember the antidote, but if we could get old Doctor
Morerod at Burnt Mountain over the phone he
would be sure to know.

After some delay Peter repeated Doctor Morerod's
reply verbatim. He said: "Tell those blamed fools
to give her a pint of olive oil and a pint of vinegar."
The druggist proudly produced the oil. "The
vinegar?" cried Peter. "Wal, I don't know 'bout
thet," said the caretaker. "The stores is all shet,
but maybe we kin drive round ter Faulkner's and
git him ter open up." It was all so absurd that, as
my throat refused to laugh, my face wore such a
sardonic grin I feared the druggist would administer
the antidote for strychnine, from symptoms!

On the way home the caretaker said suspiciously,
"'Pears like you-all is pow'ful ca'm! Most folks
likes ter live," and I knew he thought I had attempted suicide.

"Who is this Doctor Morerod?" asked Peter.

"Why, he 's a feller thet come ter Burnt Mounting a long time ago. He 's got more books 'n inybody in the world, and I holped haul a pie-anner plum up the mounting fur him."

Occasionally we came upon these "furriners" hidden away in the mountains. Fugitives from reality, or from memory; or fugitives from the law, "furriners" forever, but safe with people who look upon "a reasonable killin'" as a venial sin.

One day we met a mountaineer who was walking to the penitentiary to visit his brother. He said with rather an air of importance, "Bud war a good boy — jist too high-sperited. Pappy tutored him a lot, but hit did n't do no good. He war thet high-sperited, the second man he shot they cotched him."

Monday morning I declared that I was able to take the road again. We were restive in the cabin, for it rained Sunday and the scent of peach culls was over-powering. After an hour on the highway there was a sweet shaded way leading south. White sand as clean and unmarked as a wave-washed beach, where the late muscadines fell from their separate stems like big purple beads from a broken strand. After the querulous voices of tired men, after the insolent warnings of motors with their poisonous breath, the blessed silence, broken only by the mourning of the wood dove, whose hollow grieving holds no note of earthly bitterness or rebellion. After the acid scent of decaying fruit, the clean smell of the pines and the pungent perfume of pennyroyal hot in the sun. We walked slowly, stopping to catch our breath at the scarlet flash of a cardinal's wing, or to lean against a gray rock where a passion vine climbed, lifting a white cross above its purple, silken-fringed altar cloth. Often for days we wandered on in enchanted silence, exchanging only necessary words for provisions at crossroad stores, our only adventure the quick trenching, perhaps, of our little tent before a storm, when we would all huddle together, John's tail sometimes waving in the water of the trench, and sleep soundly with never a thought of a cold. These were halcyon days; though, when adventure beckoned, we followed with zest.

This was to be a day of simple happenings, which to us were thrilling adventures; for there, laving his feet in a crystal stream running busily across the road, sat a young man in riding breeches and coat, with a pair of high boots beside him into which he was sprinkling foot-ease. Leaning against a sweet-gum tree was a lank mountaineer, with a book, evidently a Bible, in his hand. The two were in animated conversation. We asked for a spring for a drink, and the mountaineer said, "Hit 's good water jist above whar he 's washin' his feet." We drank slowly and stopped to listen. The hiker went on in a loud contentious voice, "But no man is such a fool as to deny the evolution of animal life, even if he is idiot enough to claim special creation for man!"

"I reckon," drawled the mountain man, "thet I 'm jist thet sort of a igit. I want ter make my posi-

tion clar. I believe thet whin God wanted ter make
a man He made a man; and whin He wanted ter
make a bug, He made a bug."

"Ha, ha, ha! And when He wanted a chigger
He made this God-awful bug that's boring into my
leg! What infernal rot! All because an obscene old
history of one of the tribal gods of the Jews is read
by the ignorant. Science, of course, is a closed book
to the fools!"

The mountaineer paled beneath his tan, but he said
quietly, "Yes, suh, I'm ignerant, and you're eddicated, and you've read a lot of highfalutin books.
But whin did one o' thim science books ever comfort
a broken heart, er change a bad man suddent inter a
good man? This old Bible does jist thet! Bless
the Lord!"

"Bless the Lord!" cried Peter.

"Amen, brother!" shouted the mountaineer.

"Amen!" I added solemnly.

"Nonsense!" cried the hiker. "That old Bible
makes a man a coward and a hypocrite! And a
broken heart had better quit. Don't let the fools
breed. Let the weaklings die off and make way for
a race above good and evil!"

At this, to him, utterly devilish proposal, the
mountaineer's jaw dropped, and his fingers clenched
white on his Book.

Peter, fearing a Holy War would break out in the
mountains, said quickly to the hiker, who was lacing
his boots, "Stranger, thim hain't the sort o'shoes to

wear. Yore feet needs air. We jist wear moccasins, — carry a extry pair, — and we ben walkin' all summer and hain't had no foot trouble. Thar hain't no snakes in ther road. We jist saw one all summer." I gazed on Peter with pride, and we all went on together.

Suddenly from nowhere came the sound of a fiddle. "Is n't that 'Billy in the Low Ground'?" I asked.

"That 's Billy," Peter answered. And presently we came upon a house where there was a group of men on the porch. It was a "big dinner," celebrating Grandpap's ninetieth birthday, and Grandpap himself was playing, his gnarled old fingers finding their way straight to the heart of "Billy in the Low Ground."

After a while I produced my Villaume violin, which they handled curiously, with its unheard-of chin rest. One after another of the men played, but I knew better than to compete, for, try as I would, I could not master the art. A mountain player holds his fiddle firmly against his side, and plays with only a few inches of his bow. He tunes anew for any change of key, and it is a "sorry player" who observes a rest or a pause. The fiddler blends his whole being in the monotonous swing, as sweet and sure and incessant as the rhythm of falling water. Deep in the gayest tunes he plays there is, to me, an undertone of sadness, — the spirit of the mountains, — as irrevocable and as inevitable as death. Fancy, perhaps. But America would lose much should the art die out.

An anæmic lad of about fourteen tuned an especially vicious fiddle. But he muted it with his knife blade and played well up on the finger board with his clawlike hands. "The Land of the Cloudless Sky" rang out true and sweet, and wonderfully appealing. I gave him a mute. He had never seen one, and I shall never forget his delight. The boy had the God's gift, and I left him next morning playing the Rubinstein "Melody in F," with his first long bow. But I had to assure his mammy, Miss Laura, that it was a church tune. For, Miss Laura said, "Ralph 's goin' ter be a preacher. He don't play only church tunes."

I ate with the women at the "second table." The mountain men eat first, the women waiting. They approach the table as a filling station for renewal of energy. To speak, except for food, is a gaucherie, and as embarrassing as a loud voice when music unexpectedly ceases. Peter said he did not dare offer Grandpap many happy returns, though there was the wherewithal for a toast.

While Miss Laura, who seemed terribly efficient, was "dishin' up," I asked my neighbor at dinner which man was the father of Miss Laura's talented boy. She answered me, with a portion of chess pie poised on her knife: "Ralph hain't got no pappy. He 's a woods colt. His pappy wuz a preacher, though. He come hyar frum Nashville with lung trouble. He died. Miss Laura she 's mighty feared fur Ralph. He wears a flannel waist, and she keeps the winders shet summer and winter whar he sleeps. She 's goin' ter make a preacher of him."

"How fine!" I said inanely. I was thinking of the attitude of these simple people toward illegitimacy. For in the mountains a woman's sacred duty is to bear a child — preferably in wedlock, but a child is a child.

The next morning we set out for Wildcat Dam, "the lonesomest place in the mountings, whar thar is two houses and the best fishin' in the world." We met no one, although there were moonshine caches along the way. We had learned to read the signs, like gypsy patrins, of fresh boughs where we could follow a dim path and, putting a quarter on a stump and turning our backs, find a good drink of corn liquor.

It was late afternoon when we came to a grassy cove hemmed in close by mountains. A ruined water mill added a sadness to the scene. Across a wide rushing river stood the old dam, and from its crenate wall dozens of vipers obtruded their flattened heads and forked tongues, their lidless eyes looking down on the foaming water below. Peter stopped to shoot at them, and I walked on by the river road to find a house. For the place oppressed me, and I craved a camp this night near friendly human beings. The river sang a haunting song. Old memories waked and cried, and conquered griefs woke to fight again.

But when I came upon a white house with a long gallery where, on a rustic chair, lay an open book, I called myself names, and reflected that I was tired. For walking down a mountain is harder muscle-work than climbing.

Through an open screened door I saw a neat room where a scholarly-looking man, with jetty hair pushed back from a noble forehead, sat delicately leafing a book. A stack of books and magazines was piled at his side. I knocked and knocked again, but the man never looked up or ceased his careful leafing of his book. Concluding that the man was deaf, I called, for, through another room, I saw two women sitting on a porch before a little garden gay with hollyhocks and zinnias. A young woman, with the same intellectual beauty of the reading man, came and, in a beautifully modulated, full-throated voice, bade me enter. The reading man never looked up from his book. A woman of the type once called motherly sat stringing beans, and a curly-haired boy of six, perhaps, played with a kitten. I sat and helped string the beans and talked of ourselves. The place was neat, like a New England home. For the Southern home aims at beauty rather than order and convenience. After a while I said, "Though we are camping, I wonder if you would take us to board a few days, while I fish." And, fearing a recrudescence of sadness, I added, "I believe I could be happy here."

The woman called softly, "Father! Father!" and

from another room appeared the most gigantic man I had ever seen. His fiery eyes were set in a finely modeled head utterly destitute of a single hair. "Father," said the woman, "here is a lady who wants to stop with us a few days. She says she thinks she might be happy here."

The old man offered me his mighty hand. He said, "If you think you can be happy here, stay a day or a year." I thanked him; and the young woman — sullenly, I thought — showed me a room with dainty curtains and hooked rugs and oh, bliss! an outside bathroom with a row of white towels! I hastened away with the joyful news.

But at the door the woman stopped me. "I must tell you," she said, "there is a reason why you may not like to stop with us. My son, here, is what they call an idiot. He is quite harmless, but people are afraid of him."

"You mean," I cried, "the scholarly gentleman reading?"

"He has leafed books like that for forty years. He never tears or soils a book, and he'll cry if we take them away. He is as helpless as a baby, and I've never left him day or night for forty-three years."

I leaned against the screen and looked at the man in his long clean Russian blouse, leafing his book with dainty care. And I, in my insolent egoism, had asked these people to take me in that *I* might be happy! Suddenly the man looked up and wailed in a long descending cadence the word "*F-l-y!*" "It's the only word he can say," said his mother, "and he 'll say it till I catch the fly." And incessantly he sang the word until the fly was caught!

We stepped outside and a man rattled up in a wagon. He called, "I 'll be pow'ful obleeged ef you-all 'll jist ask Charlie to step outside and see ef hit 's goin' ter rain. I 've got ter cut hay, and don't wanter hev hit down in the rain." The woman led her son gently to the porch. He stood a moment like a sage in profound meditation. Then his body began to sway, and his arms waved like a tree in the distress of storm, and his voice rose like the sough of the wind until it was unbearable.

"Much obleeged!" said the man. "I won't cut hay till after the storm."

"He always knows when it will rain, and people come for miles around to consult him," the mother said proudly. Astonished, I asked her what sign he made if it was to be clear. "He dances as light, and makes the prettiest sound — like bees murmuring."

Peter came up the road, and I beckoned him. It was curious to watch John's attitude toward the imbecile. He stared and cringed, and fixed his eyes on the man as though he saw forms invisible to us. During our three days' stay John haunted him, staring transfixed before the idiot, who never lifted his eyes. A youth of an inferior type came in and was introduced as the husband of Emma, the daughter. And I observed that the child feared and disliked him.

After supper, — and what white linen and what a dainty tea cozy! — while Peter admired the grandfather's clock, I looked curiously at the books, remarking on the many books of travel.

"Yes," said our host, "I am an Englishman. I was a sailor, and was wrecked on the coast of Africa. That's where I got this bald head. Three of us got to shore, but the other two died on the way. They picked me up crazy with fever. When I woke in a native hut there was n't a hair on my head."

"But how," I asked, "did you find this remote place?"

"I shipped for America and found my wife here. I bought the finest wig in Boston to win her," he laughed. "I wear it now on our anniversary days."

"I am English too," said his wife, "but I came to America as a child. Father was always hankering for the sea, so we came here to be out of the sight and sound of the water."

And in my Pollyanna way I said, "But you have found peace and quiet here."

The old man smiled at me sadly. "A man's fate is written on his forehead. He can't sidestep his destiny. You are looking at those Correspondence Courses. I had to educate my children here, so I just learned along with them. Emma can read French as well as she can English."

"You have other children?" I asked.

"Yes, two sons," he said shortly.

That night there was a violent storm and a tree crashed down near our window. I thought of Charlie, and I marveled. I marvel still.

I sat on the porch, tired from fishing — but what a string of bass I caught! The woman brought her sewing and sat with me. "The little white building opposite, perched on the mountain side — a church?" I asked.

"Yes, but I can't bear the sight of it. That's why my flower garden's on the other side."

"Forgive me — I did n't know."

Then the woman began to speak, slowly and with difficulty, the words released with effort — slow drops from an old wound that bleeds afresh.

"The boy's father preached at that church. He's not Ed's child. His father came from the city to help in the spring and fall revivals. Emma sang in his choir — she is a beautiful singer. All my children have good voices. When the spring revival was over he went away. After a while I knew the truth. He promised to marry her when he came back in the fall. But he never wrote, and he did n't give her his address. When he came back he never came near her. (He used to come home with her from the Class — they call their choir that.) She tried to see him, but he would n't see her. I did n't dare tell Father. He has an insane temper when he's roused. Oh, I was afraid! He idolized Emma. You see, they kind of grew up together with their learning books, and reading. She was n't like she is now. Always singing and roaming the mountains with Robert and Edward. Robert was twenty-three and Edward was twenty-one. Emma was just eighteen. They were so proud of her."

The woman rocked to and fro and wrung her hands. "If only I had n't told them! But I did! I did! They went to the man and tried to make him marry Emma. But he threatened to have them arrested. He said he scarcely knew her. Everyone would have been against us. You see, we are 'furriners' and Father did n't like their dissenters' church. My boys took the money from under the fireplace, — the money they 'd saved, — and saddled their horses and took their guns. I tried to hold them. It was dark. Emma had walked on to church. But they kissed me good-bye — it was the last time I ever saw them!"

I reached over and took the woman's hand.

"Father went to sleep. I sat out here in the dark, watching the lights of the church, waiting — waiting. Charlie was restless and would n't sleep. He kept walking up and down in the dark, calling to the storm. Sometimes I thought I 'd call Father, but I did n't dare. The old clock ticked so slow — so slow! It struck eleven as they sang their last song. It was 'Just As I Am' — they sing it often and I turn sick when the breeze brings it! Then there were two shots — quick — one after the other. They had sung in the Class, my two boys; then they got their guns and as he came out the door they both shot. They loved each other — they did n't want either to bear the blame alone."

"Oh, tell me they escaped!" I cried. I thought I could not bear it if they had not got away!

"Robert did. It 's been six years. We 've never heard from him. But Edward is in the penitentiary. Father goes to see him. He won't live long. I can't leave Charlie to go. Ed worked for us and he offered to marry Emma. I begged her not to. But they — Father and Emma — wanted the child born in wedlock. But Ed hates the boy, and Emma hates him. I 'm afraid! There 's more trouble to come! Sometimes I wish she 'd leave the boy with me and run away. But what will become of Charlie when Father and I go? He could never bear harsh or coarse treatment. Charlie is an idiot, I know — but he 's *refined!*"

As we walked on the next day, Peter said: "And all that tragedy because they brought their old-fashioned standards here! Why, Emma could have been the Miss Laura of the settlement!"

"But," I cried from a heavy heart, "there remains always Charlie! Forty-three years! Never a day away!"

We took the highway to the county seat, for we had a traveler's check to cash. Six miles from the town we came upon a church set on a hill overlooking a wide valley. Peter wanted to walk on. He said he was about fed up with preachers. But I said that we must n't generalize; that predatory preachers did not alight in flocks; that I was wickedly "sunk," and needed the innocent exaltation of their simple piety. So we camped by the little churchyard with its small white stones and red roses, and made ourselves fine for evening service. The congregation was already assembling, and we were told it was a big meeting, and the finest preacher from the city was helping. A slender youth, his white sleeves billowing in the evening breeze, stood on the steps of the church overlooking the shadowed valley and sounded the call to prayer on a shining bugle. He played the reveille, then taps, and it was all very beautiful, and peace descended on my troubled spirit.

Two men approached us, one carrying a Bible. We knew by his locked face, his controlled gestures, and his public voice that one was the city preacher. Without a word of greeting, he said: "What are you people traveling on? What are you selling?" We answered, "Nothing." "Well, you move on!" he cried. "We can't have you here distracting the minds of these young folks. There are souls to be saved here this night! Move on!"

We insinuated that we had no intention of putting on a rival show, that we had walked far, and that we only desired to hear him preach. But he cried, angrily, "Move on! We don't want you here. Godless tin-can tourists are enough in this country, without tramps! Move on!"

Peter said, "As to what we are traveling on, I can't see that it is your business, but we are traveling on what, evidently, you are preaching for — money."

The man's face was convulsed with rage. "Here!" he called to a group of young people listening eagerly. "Follow these tramps out of our neighborhood."

Peter had gone for John and the cart; and I said, unwisely, "We are glad to go on, for the spirit of your Master is not here, as I 'll tell everyone we meet."

"Don't you dare tell I drove you away from this church!" he cried. "We can't have loafers about attracting attention. If you had been selling something useful you might have stayed. Move on!"

We stumbled on in the dark, followed by a jeering crowd. But the country preacher called, in a voice of authority, "Don't you pester them people! And whin the horn plays you turn right back — iver' one of you!" And the sad young man at Locksley Hall never heard his comrades "sound upon the bugle horn" with greater relief than we felt when "Come to Jesus! Come to Jesus!" called suddenly through the night.

I walked on so rapidly that Peter objected. "I am fleeing from the Christians!" I cried. "I know how the Moors felt when the Christians had them at water's edge!"

It was now pitch-dark, and we were tired and tempted to make camp. But we reminded ourselves that later the road would be filled with zealots, their inferiority complexes ironed out and their egotism

inflated, and we might not be safe. At last we came
to the little city, where only a friendly night watch-
man was awake. He directed us to the schoolhouse
yard to camp, and we crept next a bed of blooming
cannas by an open window and slept the sleep of
exhaustion.

I awoke with the sun in my eyes, to find Peter with
a pitcher of hot tea. He was laughing uproariously.
"Where do you think we are?" he cried. "This is
the city preacher's church, and this is his study
window! And Lord, how they hate him here!"
While Peter packed hurriedly, — the parsonage was
next door, — with childish glee I wrote a bread-and-
butter letter, tied it to a pebble by a fishing line, and
swung it until it alighted in the middle of the fat Bible
on the city preacher's desk. I wrote: —

REVEREND SIR: —
This is to thank you for the hospitality of your canna
bed, where we slept and breakfasted. Your neighbors ask
that you preach next Sabbath from the text about enter-
taining angels unawares. (I have n't the verse and
chapter, but no doubt you can find it.) We are buying
the truth and selling it not.

Yours in brotherly love,

THE TRAMPS

"Now," I said proudly, "let 's inquire for the
blackest moonshine belt, where we 'll be safer."

VII

THE RIVER ROAD

WE tied John to the wheel of Sisyphus and pushed
the cart into the deep shadow of the white frame
church with its top-heavy belfry. Then we spread
our tattered road map on the steps of the church for
the ever-delightful conference as to where the day
should call us.

As usual, the inhabitants of the remote mountain
village gathered about us. The hounds and coon
dogs, less polite than the mountaineers, began to
question John. As always when he is tied, John
waved his white-plumed tail and gazed at the far
horizon in contemptuous silence.

Ordinarily there was small need of the map. For,
drifting before the wind of destiny, we ever chose the
most unfrequented way, with the wind preferably at

our backs. But this day there was need of drifting toward a bank where we could cash the last one of our modest traveler's checks. Peter was of the opinion that we had spent them all; but a cursory glance in the chamois bag at my neck revealed one more little crisp paper. And we had but forty-five cents left in money. Sis's bicycle wheels would break on rocky trails and must be mended or replaced; shoes, and especially stockings, would wear out; and there was always the temptation to buy some useless article from a mountain woman, whose hard fingers touched a piece of silver as reverently and as curiously as one might touch a rare jewel.

The highway to the right of the Hard Shell Baptist Church evidently led to the county seat. For there men with mules jogged along, and motor cars whizzed past them. Peter, with relief, pointed out on the map that, while there was a bank at the county seat, there was no railway. But I hated the rock-crushed highways where once I had seen the convicts work, and at the left of the church there wound a dusty, shaded way toward the river. Beyond, skirting the mountain above, I saw it turn and twine toward the west, where the county seat lay. I pleaded for the river road.

It was in vain that Peter pointed out to me that when one started on a journey it was usual to set forth in the direction of the place where one expected to arrive. But I felt sure that the river road would eventually arrive at the town, and even suggested

that we ask one of the women who gaped about us.
For some reason there was not a man to be seen in
the village. Of course I knew that it was hopeless
to ask the way of a mountain woman. She would
answer kindly, "That-air road runs ter Grandpap
Bryant's."

"And from there ?"

"I hain't niver ben no furder. I don't know whar
hit might go frum thar."

"Peter," I cried, "there is a man in the little yard
opposite."

"It 's a woman."

"It 's a man. He has on a veil, because he is
working with his bees. He is taking honey from the
hives."

We folded our precious map and started to push
Sisyphus across the grass-grown road. A gaunt
woman wearing a purple sunbonnet leaned toward me
and said, "I reckon you-all don't wanter go over thar.
Mr. Jackson lives thar. Ther hain't nobody iver
goes thar. He 's er infi-*del*."

I thanked her and assured her that we only meant
to ask about the road. Peter called across the picket
fence before the log cabin so small it seemed the
capital of a little city of beehives : "Good morning.
May I trouble you with a question ?"

The man came out through the swinging gate, took
off his heavy gloves, and removed his veil. I
watched curiously his sensitive, eloquent hands. He
wore khaki and leggings. Forty-five, perhaps,

smooth-shaven, tall, slender, with bent shoulders; we looked on, not into, his opaque brown eyes.

"Yes?" he said in a rusty voice, and walked slowly around the cart, where, in large white letters, "Sisy" was painted on one green side and "-phus" on the other. Then his creaking voice went on, "Well, Sisyphus, don't ask me how to keep your cursed wheel from slipping back."

We were too astonished to speak at once. For in all our wanderings through the mountains no one of the many who had gazed wonderingly at our Chinese wheelbarrow had ever connected the words on its sides.

At last Peter said, "No? Mrs. Sisyphus wishes to know if the river road eventually arrives at the county seat. And I want to ask if this is an Adamless Eden. I have n't seen a man in the village."

"Will you walk into the house and rest a moment?" said the man. "I must replace the super on my beehive. Then I 'll come in and answer your questions."

He led the way around the cabin, and I saw with surprise that there was neither door nor window in the front of his house.

"I have my entrance at the back," he said, "because I don't care to face that blast of frozen music across the road. Perhaps you noticed the jack pot of a belfry."

"Why, yes," I answered, very much amused. "But the Hard Shells have the advantage with their

jack pot. At home we 'd have to send for the bishop
to open it up."

"At home?" he said, looking at me curiously.
"But here we can never ring for a cold deck. The
cards are marked, and it 's the same old game of graft
as — at home."

Then to Peter, "Selling Bibles? Or a traveling
evangelist?"

"Unfortunately, neither," answered Peter.

"Pardon me. I 'll go in and tie Lucifer. He 's
not used to visitors."

We passed through a tiny vestibule, very clean,
with a cookstove, a table, and a solitary chair on one
side, and on the other side shelves piled high with
labeled buckets, evidently honey for shipment.
There was but one chair in the room beyond, a rustic
easy-chair on whose cushion lay a fat fox terrier, who
snarled, but made no objection to being tied to a
chain fastened to the wall. The man dusted the
cushion and offered Lucifer's throne to me. Then,
from the step of a rude stairway that ran to a loft
above, he pushed aside a coffeepot of pamphlets and
a large stewpan of magazines, invited Peter to be
seated, and went to his bees.

On the table beside me was a large oil lamp and an
open book. Bergson! Strange infidel! The walls
were lined to the ceiling with books. The floor was
mounded with books in neat piles or boxes. Under
the window was a large tin wash boiler that Peter said
was full of Plato. Through the door opposite me I

saw the only other room of the cabin. It was clean
and bare, with a snowy bed; and among the toilet
articles on the bureau stood a framed picture. As
I rose to examine the bookshelves, I confess I stole a
glance at the faded, full-length photograph of a young
woman in old-fashioned evening dress.

"Now what can I do for you?" asked the man,
appearing at the door. "As to the men of the village,
they have all gone to a murder trial at the county
seat. It is their happy carnival."

"I suppose you could n't leave the bees," said
Peter, curiously.

"I might care for a good fresh murder. In fact,
I wish I had been present at this one. But a judicial
murder does n't appeal to me. There is no charm
of the unexpected."

"So sure of the verdict?" asked Peter.

"Oh, yes. The murdered man was a preacher;
the avenger a village half-wit. I am a village atheist.
Fellow feeling, perhaps. It 's not at all a pretty
story — the half-wit's daughter. Madame Sisyphus
will not care for the tale."

"Can we reach the county seat by the river road?"
I asked.

"Yes, in time. But the river road runs through
the Indian and negro settlements."

"Indians! Here?" cried Peter.

"Not a tribe. Just scattered through the settlement. The Eastern band of Cherokees. Wandered
over from the Qualla Reservation in North Carolina.

The people here call them 'the blue men.' As a
matter of fact they look as though they might have
a mixture of negro blood — but they have not."

"Of course we must take the river road!" I cried.
"But negroes! I don't think we have seen a negro
in the mountains."

"No. The negroes in the mountains are like the
Indians — just shadows of the past. The young
negroes are off to the cities. The poor whites here
hate them, these shadows who slip in and out of the
village for supplies. They are thriftier than the
whites. A larger per cent of negroes own their own
homes in America than do whites."

"But of course the whites own their own homes
here," said Peter.

"Why, no. The storekeeper often owns their
homes through duebills — the credit system."

"Why does n't he get the negro too?"

"When the negro goes broke he goes down in the
rich valley and works for someone till he can carry
on."

The man's voice, as if oiled by use, took on cultivated modulations, and so full and round it was
that I wondered if he were English. But I ventured
no impertinent questions, fearing what might come
alive behind those dead eyes. He said no more, and
I fancied that his glance rested longingly on the open
book beside me. No doubt we were shadows, dis-
turbing shadows. His real world was in his books.
So I rose to go, and asked him if we might buy a small

jar of the honey. Peter gave me a warning glance that said, "Forty-five cents." But I murmured, "We 'll spend it like a prince for the stored-up sweetness of this summer's flowers."

"Humph!" said Peter unsympathetically.

The man returned with a little bucket carefully wrapped, and said, "Permit me, Madame Sisyphus." And only when he had refused the money did Peter's face relax.

Our host walked a little way with us, and I noticed the curious halt in his step.

Outside the village we met the woman of the purple sunbonnet.

"The man, Mr. Jackson — has he been here long?" I asked.

"Tin yar ergo hit war whin he kim hyar, and bought ther house by ther church and turned hit eround. He war hurted in his laig. Some sez he 's lakin'. But I 'low he jest sulls. He air a infi-*del*."

"Ah," said Peter as we walked on, "his limp — the lock step, perhaps. Poor devil!"

"Oh, no!" I cried. "He 's lame. Recall what he said about the murder trial. He just refuses to share the guilt of the world with the rest of us. The religionists do it in another way. Our sins ought to hold us together. We grow queer on the heights. Poor lonely infi-*del!* His books are his opium!"

The river road! Cool golden sands beneath white-armed sycamores. The river road, where solemn cows converse disparagingly about us, and dispute

our right of way; where mules look over the rail
fences through their wise, bitter eyes; where the
sudden print of a child's bare foot in the sand is a
great work of art; where a tawny bobcat, intent on
his own business, trots across on noiseless padded
feet, at once another shadow in the sun-flecked wood.
Where cardinals flash from green bird-haunted
thickets, and a friendly mocking bird cools his wing in
the clear water of the ford where we stop a moment
to fish.   Where the fitful breeze brings the languorous
sweetness of the honeysuckle, and John selects the
ripest of the plump black dewberries by the wayside,
and deserts them when a red squirrel — a very short
expression of life with a question mark at the end —
runs up a sweet gum, and we leave John in acute
hysteria at the foot of the tree.   Where a wagon with
bolt timber creaks slowly down the hill, and we stand
before the cart that the mules may not shy; and the
driver stops, and three other log wagons stop, and
we all meet on the common ground of the weather
with abundant time to exhaust the subject.   For a
highway is but a way of transit, as dangerous and as
monotonous as a railway track, but a country road is
a pleasant retreat where "all the world" may meet
in careless leisure.

Beside the jade-green river the road ran in and
out, then up and up the mountain.   And when we
came to a little knoll deep in pine needles, with a clear
spring gushing at its foot, we made our noon camp,
and broiled our two fat perch.

Though we had seen cabins at a distance, we had met no Indians, no negroes.

"These Indians, the blue men, are probably creoles," said Peter as he lay on the pine needles smoking his after-dinner cigarette. I replied that I hoped they were, for I loved the creoles; meaning not the French creoles so familiar to us in New Orleans, but the miscalled creoles of the rural districts in the Gulf States — a mixture of negro and Indian.

Peter laughed, as he always did when he thought of our first acquaintance with the creoles.

It was one day when I was seated sullenly on the verandah of a deserted hotel near the railway station of a little town where we waited to connect with a road that ran to another tedious town on the Gulf. These towns were all alike. I was weary of the glaring water and the voice of the realtor in the land. I desired dully, like a lotus-eater, never more to roam — even in search of health. Peter had gone across the street to get me a cup of coffee. A tall, lank man with blue soot-rimmed eyes leaned against a pillar and said, "The train is late to-day."

"Yes," I answered; "I have heard no excited rumors that it is on time. But I don't care if it never comes."

"Don't you want to go on?"

"No."

"Where do you want to go?"

"I want to go," I answered dreamily, "away from the sea waves. I want to go to a blue river where green banks come down to the water's edge; and below low hills boats — only little boats — glide silently. But I 'm describing another country — Paradise, maybe."

"Why, no. It 's about seven miles from here. Have you bought your tickets?"

"No."

"I can't get away until two o'clock. But you can wait over at the Mitchell House. At two I 'll come and take you over there. Any baggage?"

"Two suitcases. Here are the checks. But I think we 'll walk on toward Paradise and lunch by the roadside. You can pick us up in the car. I 'll tie a handkerchief to a tree or something if we are far from the road."

So when Peter came with the coffee the man told him our destination, and we hastened joyfully to buy bread, bacon, cakes, and tea, and started for Paradise.

But Jordan is a hard road to travel. At noon, after innumerable cups of tea over a little camp fire, a storm, utterly unheralded, broke, and we rushed to a ruined, deserted house near us. For half an hour the wind blew a hurricane. The left wing of the house collapsed, and sent a horde of rats upon us. But the storm ceased suddenly, the sun shone, and the car honked from the road. In a few minutes we stopped before a tiny cottage where the yard waved with phlox of varied hues in lieu of grass. I sat under a great umbrella tree while Peter and our friend went to find the landlord. But the landlord was shooting 'gator bait. His wife told them that the 'gators were rather bad. One had climbed on the bank, hit a sheep with its tail, and carried it into the river, just where the children bathed. So they were to put out bait and torches, and shoot him in the eye this night. But she found the key, and the little house was clean and comfortable; and oh, the beautiful cedar ceilings and walls! Our friend, disclaiming all money or thanks, drove away, saying he would come Sunday to see how we liked it.

Liked it! Feeble words! We set off at once down the path to the broad blue river, where, below low green hills that sloped to the water's edge, little boats drifted aimlessly about. The people stopped in the middle of the river for afternoon gossip. It was the village highway — Venice before the motor boat. A child sang as he pushed his boat across from the one store, with a loaf of bread under his arm. A fat, jolly priest tucked up his frock and poled across with a basket of eggs. Were we in America?

That night on a little wharf in a deserted garden, as we sat under a bright moon, suddenly there floated down the river a cry, melodious, penetrating, infinitely sweet. Another voice echoed, another, and far down the shining river another, until the warm moist night was vocal. The captain of the little boat at the pier stopped before us to light his pipe, and said, "The creoles are yodeling to-night. Beautiful, is n't it?"

Oh, beautiful! Not the crystal call of the Tyrolese, a cry to the god of the hills, but a cry as native as the gurgle of their river, as seductive as the perfume of the night-blooming flowers where the water laps the shore — the old, old cry to the god of the valleys.

The next morning the fish wagon stopped at our door, and I met my first creole. Lithe, dark, erect — an Arab with the mellifluous voice of the negro and the proud reserve of the Indian. When I came to know this man well, he told me that his father, a creole and a widower, had married a negress, a widow with children. Now there are three free schools — one for the whites, one for the creoles, and one for the negroes. He himself went to the creoles' school, his step-brothers to the negroes'. But when children came to this couple the threat of utter illiteracy hung over them, for all schools rejected them. After years of heated discussion, the disgrace was divided between the two schools; the children went half a term to each.

Some of the creole women, of mixed white blood, are very beautiful. A white man of means married one of these women, and on their wedding journey to Chicago the Southern railway conductor refused to permit the bride to ride in the Pullman or to allow the man in the negro coach! Though in the South we hold miscegenation in peculiar horror, yet the harm was already done, and I have always hoped that Charon made this conductor cross the Styx in the steerage.

Now, as we lay on the mountainside and recalled all this, I said, "And oh, remember the day when the mail carrier tied our skiff behind his motor boat to deliver the mail!" For here was the only rural river route in America. Against the law to take us? But in this languorous land how far away the law seems! And the creoles sauntered silently down green banks to their little wharves, and there among the water lilies we gave them their letters without a word to break the steady swish-swish of the reeds.

So, lighting one cigarette after another from the dying fire, we "tired the sun with talking and sent him down the sky."

Unnoticed, an ominous cloud had appeared in the west, and we hastened for the camp shovel to trench for the tent, and prepared for the night on the hill.

That night John gave the man-growl, and the next morning as I boiled the tea while Peter foraged for wood — pine does not make a cooking fire — I saw behind the golden splash of Spanish needle a man creeping away in the bushes. The storm still threatened, and we dug the trench deeper and stayed another night; though John, who did not like the hill, begged to go on. The following morning, as Peter cleared the trench for the still threatening storm, again I saw the man in the bushes. I took the rifle and handed it quietly to Peter, and told him to look. Peter pointed the gun at the man and cried, "Come out, friend! We don't like visitors on all fours!"

An Indian with a slight blue cast — like the terror of my childhood, a man who had taken a medicine for epileptic fits — came forward calmly and said, "You are an Indian."

I looked at Peter with a fresh eye. We did look like Indians! For we were bronzed deep by the sun, and our hair hung black and long, — at least Peter's was black, — for somewhere in the cart the scissors were lost. From months of walking in moccasins we had acquired the Indian glide — and oh, the ease it brought in walking!

So Peter answered diplomatically, "Maybe."

"You are digging for our treasure — our gold. We won't let you take it. We know it is here on this hill somewhere. You can't take it. But," and a look of cunning came into his immobile face, "if you divide with me, I 'll not tell. Divide with me?"

"I 'm not digging for treasure," said Peter. "I 'm trenching our tent because it 's going to rain."

The Indian shook his head stubbornly. "Divide with me? We won't let you take our gold. I 'll not tell. When the moon shines I 'll come. Divide with me?"

"You can dig alone. I 'll not be here to-night. If you know the treasure is here, why have n't you found it?"

"The Quallas know where it is. There is gold — much gold. I 'll help you dig when the moon shines to-night." And he glided away.

We broke camp at once, so that we might not be

suspected of having found gold — much gold; though when Peter reflected on the forty-five cents he said he would like to fortify the hill and dig.

"If you ask me," he said as we walked away, "these shadows of the past are too dense to be comfortable, or I 'm an Indian!"

Though the houses of the blue men were neat and well cared for, — gardens always in front, and not a flower, — I was glad when we came to the first ramshackle negro cabin, where the hens scratched contentedly in gardens at the back and cockscombs and zinnias bloomed at the doorstone, where the pickaninnies grinned. But on the way we talked with some of the Indians and admitted that they were intelligent and thrifty.

A sad, a silent people, these lost Cherokees. Unlike the negroes, who hide their melancholy with marvelous secrecy, these Indians carry their sadness like a banner.

The clouds cleared away, and a perfume not of flowers or of ripening fruit came on the breeze — a fascinating odor to hungry wanderers. And around a turn of the road was a party of negroes before a barbecue fire. I turned into the big gate before an unexpectedly commodious house.

"But they are negroes!" said Peter doubtfully.

"That is why we shall get a good clean dinner!"

"But negroes! And we have only forty-five cents!"

"Nonsense!" I cried impatiently and unjustly.

For Peter had not been brought up in a land where
Aunt Becky kept track of your "ka-reer" through
absent years, and walked ten rheumatic miles when
you came home, to see if "you still favored yo'
paw"!

A very old white-headed negro came to greet us.
Resolved to be economical, I said, "Good morning,
Uncle. That barbecued meat smelled so good I just
had to stop and see if you would sell us a slice."

"Suhtinly! Suhtinly! Rose, cut de lady a nice
slice. One ob de blue min tole us dey wuz trablers
on de road. But you is not whut we expected teh
see, suh. Not atall, suh!"

A negress, who turned two kids on spits before an
open fire, began to sharpen a knife. Suddenly the
old man cried, "Heah, you twins! Woodrow!
You an' Sambo! Come holp me cahy obeh somethin'. Wait a minute, Miss — Miss —"

"Miss Eleanor," I answered.

"Miss Ellen," and he smiled delightedly, "you jis'
set down on de bench by de little table dar."

Presently he returned with the twins, and under a
great oak set the table with a clean white cloth and
pink-flowered dishes.

"Dese dishes," the old man said proudly, "is whut
I keeps fuh white folks comp'ny. Nobody else iveh
et in dem. I 'm ve'y much respected heah, suh. I
has a gret chance o' white comp'ny. I owns my
hunderd-acre fahm heah, suh. Ise lived heah sence
de wah wid de States. Dese folks is all my dahters

and deir chillun an' gran'chillun. Ise pow'ful ole
now. None o' my boys 'd stay on de place, an' I
wuked all my life teh make it fine fuh 'em! Dis is a
picnic fuh Rose's gal. She has a little boy baby; and
dey 's all come frum town teh bring cradle presents.
So I fotched some ice frum town, an' I barbecued
two fat kids fuh 'em."

The old negro waited on us himself, and there was
red raspberry ice cream and real pound cake. When
he had gone for more of the delicious barbecued meat,
Peter said, "How the devil are we to pay for all
this?"

"Peter," I said, "I 'm a Southern belle befo' de
wah ob de States, and you are like the man who
walked before Alexander to keep telling him he was
mortal! You and your forty-five cents! We can
get the money at the town and send it back — if
there 's not enough."

"Humph! He 'll believe that!"

Suddenly he whispered, "That little hickey you
bought of the last mountain woman — it 's a quilt,
is n't it?"

So we unlocked the cart and took from it the beautifully pieced and quilted silk square I had bought
for a footstool cover. "Uncle," I said, "may I give
the baby a cradle present too? It 's only a little
quilt, but we think it pretty."

Rose came with the other women and bore it
proudly into the house to the baby. And when we
had finished our dinner Peter, as from an inexhaust-

ible store, produced the forty-five cents and offered
it to the old negro.

"Nossuh! Nossuh! You-all is comp'ny! I kim
frum Vahginny, and my white folks wuz the Chiltons,
suh!"

Rose eyed the money covetously, and her face fell.
Her father turned to her and said sharply, "We iveh
one 'd consideh it a bodacious insult teh take money
frum a lady dat give Rose's gran'chile a fine cradle
present. We thanks you, Miss Ellen."

"Saved again!" murmured Peter.

"It 'pears lak it mought rain. I keeps one room
fuh white comp'ny. I 'd be proud if you-all would
stay."

We thanked him and declined, and he brought us
some apples to take with us. "Dey is fine apples. I
got seven kinds o' sweet apples. I planted 'em all.
But nobody keers nothin' fuh 'em. Maybe you-all
don't want 'em. I went teh Nashville teh visit my
boy an' his chillun an' gran'chillun. An' I shined
up my ve'y bestest apples I'd sprayed fo' times, an' I
wropped iveh one in fine white paper, an' I toted de
sack wid me on de kyars. But my boy he jis' th'owed
'em in de automobile an' bruised 'em. An' dat night
I calls de chillun an' I says, 'See whut you-all's ole
gran'pappy done brung you!' An' I ontied de flour
sack, an', suh, dey says, 'Nothin' but ole apples!'
An' th'owed 'em right on de flo'. Dey says dey
laks awanges, suh. It 'pears lak I done th'owed
erway all my wuk heah. Dey won't nobody even

stay on de place. Dese chillun all live in town dat 's
heah teh-day."

The old negro's eyes filled. I could not speak;
and he went on, "Miss Ellen, I hopes you won't kyar
if I axes yo' las' name. I sohteh thunk we mought
name Rose's baby boy fuh you. We kindeh runs
outen names."

I wrote my maiden name on a piece of paper, —
spelled phonetically, — and Peter said, "Cheer up!
With a name like that, this one will grow up and love
the old place and come back to it."

"I thanks you-all. You kin find a good camp in
de grove at de ole Lancaster place teh-night. De
fambly 's all gone off teh be lawyers and doctahs in
cities. But ole Miss an' little Miss is buried dar.
Little Miss's boy wuz de las' teh leave. Dar 's a
tenant dar now. Jis' pore white trash."

As we walked on, Peter said: "Now that avun-
cular shadow of the past is worth while! But those
young negroes — why, even after we gave them the
cradle present they would have taken our —"

"If you say 'forty-five cents' again I shall
scream! What have we to do with high finance?"

"You are right! The joy of the road is that the
exigencies of the present shut off the past and the
future. But the money smoulders in my pocket!
And I have a feeling that a good-sized exigency is
coming. We 'll spend it at the next stop."

After supper in the dimly lighted old hall of the
Lancaster mansion, with its pathetic spindle-legged

piano and occasional carved chair, I played the violin for the tenant and the field hands who lolled on the great stairway or sprawled on the floor. Hoping to find a mountain fiddler, I passed the violin among them. A mellow voice from the dark called, "I kin play, if de lady don't mind."

"Come in, Uncle Eli," said our host kindly. "You used ter live hyar, did n't ye?"

An old, old negro stood framed in the doorway. Neatly dressed, with hightopped boots of a bygone fashion, he stood slender and straight as a charred pine.

I caught the veiled contempt in the glance he gave the field hands sprawled about the old hall. A glance that included me in my short skirt and bobbed hair.

"Yas, suh! Yas, suh! I done sold my fiddle in dis berry hall when I went Nawth wid de fambly. I ain't played no mo'. But I done come home now, suh."

He fingered the violin lovingly with trembling old hands, and pushed the bow across the strings. But the music did not come. Sadly enough he brought it back to me. "I reckon Ise done fergot how teh play," he said.

"Try again, Uncle Eli," I said. "It will come back to you. It always does."

It did come back to him, and after he had tuned the violin in his own way he said, "I 'll play you de oldest tune in de worl'. It 's 'De Road teh Jericho.'

An' de good Book say it made de walls o' Jericho fall."

Half a century and more has passed since Old Miss sat in her hoop-skirted dress and smiled while she watched the dancers and listened to Uncle Eli's fiddle.

Old reels sparkled and lilted through the great hall; and suddenly one of the field hands sprang to his feet and cried, "Hoe all day an' hop all night!" And presently they were all dancing like mad. We hopped with the best of them. Even our host's tiny daughter joined the revels. Then, for the first time, I saw Uncle Eli smile. He sang with the violin, "Hold up youah dress an' dance lak a lady. Nobody hyah but Kitty an' de baby." The old white head so weighted with memories sank lower and lower. Perhaps he had sung that song for little Miss who sleeps under the oaks here, while her great-grand-daughter dances to jazz music at a cabaret.

Night, when the whippoorwill called incessantly in the deep grove; and before sunrise we stole silently away to meet the mystery of the dawn breeze on the river road.

When the sun was hot we stopped at a desolate cabin for a drink. Inside, a weary woman was iron-ing, heating her irons before a fireplace, while a young woman sat in a cushioned chair and crocheted with very coarse twine what she called hats. The girl was beautiful. All the expression denied her body was concentrated in her face. For she had never walked.

She was selling the hats to buy herself a wheel chair. When she told me they were fifty cents, Peter's eyes met mine, and without a word he gave me forty-five cents and three postage stamps.

Outside, to prove the wisdom of my purchase, I tried to wear the hat. But it volplaned like an airship. Even a string weighted with a rock failed to secure it. So I removed the wire at the edge, made a hand bag of it, and felt lighter in my mind.

At last we stood on the summit of a steep hill, and Peter said, "If the mists would lift we could see the bank in the town."

Sis, always of an unbalanced nature, became excited at this, and ran violently down the hill. We all three pursued, screaming and barking. A motor rattled past. We had come to the end of the river road.

VIII

VALLEY FOLKS

A MOUNTAINEER, in a speculative mood, will push back his hat, take an extra chew of tobacco, and drawl: "I don't noways aim ter shorten the power o' Gawddlemighty, but I 'low hit 'pears lak hit seems thet thar's one thing He cain't do Hisself. He cain't make two mountings 'ithout a valley atween 'em."

Peter often tossed this nugget of wisdom at me as I irrationally considered some way of avoiding valleys and valley folks on our journey with the pushcart.

It seemed preposterous that a mere protuberance on the earth's surface should so change the manners of people living but a few miles from each other. I was reminded that the way we earn our bread makes a vast difference in us; and that the people of the rich valleys earn their bread in an easier way than the mountaineers, and earn more of it. The labor of others serves the owner of valley land, and his manners — the mirror of man's relation to other men — seem to have lost the antique dignity which still distinguishes the mountain man. "For no pauper ever felt him condescend, nor Prince presume." He has no need for the nice adjustment of his relation to other men; for he knows but one class, and gives every man the respect he feels due himself.

Something of this was in my mind as we pushed Sisyphus slowly down the dusty road of the little town toward the bank where we had come to cash the last one of our traveler's checks. We were light-heartedly penniless, for I had just spent that last forty-five cents for an airy nothing in the way of a crocheted hat. But though we were in sight of funds we were tired and hungry; Sis was empty of food; and it was Saturday afternoon. So we hurried on for fear of the bank's closing early.

It was a little town with no railway. We passed pretentious places with well-cared-for grounds, and beside them neglected tumble-down shacks. In a mountain village it is true that the inhabitants would collect about us and gaze wonderingly at our Chinese wheelbarrow. But they ever regarded us with a certain compassion, knowing us to be homeless wanderers. These valley folks stared at us with hard eyes of derisive curiosity. One by one the inhabitants of the town set out after us; and, rather annoyed Pied Pipers, we trudged before them on the way to the bank.

"Give you fifty cents fur that dawg."

"Where you-all goin' ?"

"Whut you sellin' ?"

"Whut a consarned little wagon !"

"Hello, Sissy ! Goin' ter give a show ? Goin' ter preach, Sis ?"

I counted the minutes until we could get the money and climb the nearest road to the mountain. The "sweet security of streets" was not for us. Charles Lamb's ghost could n't find security in streets to-day.

The crowd, constantly augmented, followed us into the little bank, and the overflow pressed against the window. I went inside with the check, because John was in no pleasant mood, and there might be a dog fight to settle.

A solemn, pasty-faced man peered at me over his spectacles as I hurriedly reached in the chamois bag at my neck and gave him the last little crisp paper. He read it carefully, then contemptuously tossed it back to me.

"This is n't a check," he said. "It 's just the printed wrapper that comes around the checks."

I gazed at the paper in horror. It was too true. I recalled now that Peter had insisted that we had cashed them all. But I carried the checks, and there was that little paper with the formula printed thereon ! Now, disaster ! How could I face Peter, waiting so hopefully outside ?

The grinning crowd now chuckled in open amusement. "Fifty cents fur yer dawg!" "Hit the grit,
Sis!"

I longed to run to Peter and transfer this trouble
to him. But it was all my fault, so I turned to the
banker and asked him if he would telegraph to our
bankers on the Eastern Shore of Mobile.

"There is a telephone at the drug store," he said.
"You can telephone from there. We have no telegraph."

"But," I said, "I have n't any money. Could n't
you telephone and pay yourself for the trouble when
the money comes?"

"I could n't take the risk. It would cost something. Would have to be relayed twice." And he
turned away. The crowd jeered openly. You
could n't fool their banker! Cruel? No. They
were reveling in a fresh emotion, elated by the moral
elevation that comes from catching a would-be
swindler.

As I tried to push my way to the door a tall youth
bent his sunburnt face above me and said in a low
tone, "There is another bank here. A little one.
The Farmer's Bank. Try it. I 'll show you the
way."

Outside, in a few broken words, I told the tragic
tale, and we set out for the other bank — Peter, Sis,
John, and I in the middle of the street like a circus
parade; followed, I do believe, by every able-bodied
man in the town except the pasty-faced banker.

Before a little green one-roomed building, in an
easy-chair on the sidewalk, dozed a ponderous man.
He straightened up with difficulty, rubbed his eyes,
and stared at this mob descending upon him with an
air almost of fright. Our friend the youth spoke a
word to him; he heaved himself up, waddled heavily
into the room, followed by Peter, glared threateningly
at the rest of us, and slammed the door. Presently
Peter came to the window and nodded reassuringly
to me. I whispered a word to my sunburnt knight,
who stood beside me, and he pushed Sisyphus across
to the drug store. In a moment I had unlocked the
cart, tuned my violin, and climbed on the bench
before the store. I meant to pay for my carelessness
and to make this crowd pay for its impudent curiosity. So I bowed in my best manner, and said:
"My friends, I feel sure that you will be pleased to
know that the Farmer's Bank is sending for our
money. But we must live until it comes. This is
Saturday. The money will not come, perhaps, until
Monday. I intend to play for you, and I intend to
pass the hat afterward; so if anyone does n't care
to hear he may leave now. I shall spend every cent
I collect at the grocery store next door — putting
the money at once back into circulation in your
charming little city." And I dashed into what
fireworks I could command at the moment. I hoped
to finish before Peter could know, but he ran across
the street, mingled horror and amusement in his face.
I ended hastily on an improvised chord, and passed

my hat. While the crowd cheered, — more in admiration of my nerve than my music, I fear, — Peter, not to be outdone, reached in the cart for a book we had received at the last mountain post office. He stepped jauntily on the bench, and, waving the book, cried : —

"Fellow citizens. As I look into the faces of this intelligent audience, the thought comes that I can say nothing that is new to you, nothing that will interest you. But there is one late discovery that maybe some of you have not heard. This is that we are all living inside the earth instead of outside it. Korish Colony of Estero, Florida, — which we recently visited, — has proved this; at least no one has disproved it. We are all crawling around like flies inside of an empty orange skin, and the stars are in the middle of it." I pulled frantically at Peter's blouse. This was tempting fate with utter reckless-ness! "Peter!" I cried. "Stop! They 'll put us in the asylum !" But he went on : "Here where you are all conversant with the latest thought of the age, you will grasp eagerly the book called *The Cellular Universe* for the ridiculous sum of twenty-five cents ! Who wants to know that he is living inside the earth for only twenty-five cents ? Also there are pictures in it — at least there are diagrams."

A wizened old man in a black coat approached and said : "I 'll take that book." "Here you are," said Peter. "I wish I had more of them for the rest of you. But it is limited in circulation. The gentleman who bought it can explain it to you — if he can understand it. I never could. I thank you."

The temper of the crowd had changed. No longer hostile, they cheered us wildly, and the druggist insisted that we come in for ice-cream soda. I invited my friend the youth to join us, and he told us that the druggist kept the key to the schoolhouse, and that we might camp there over Sunday. We accepted thankfully, for we knew there would be no privacy in our little tent in this town. I proudly counted my money. There was one dollar and twenty-six cents. With Peter's twenty-five cents we were rich again, and we spent it all at the grocery next door.

It was well that we had the key to the schoolhouse, for sixteen men and boys sat about watching us at supper by our camp fire, and I doubt if we could have slept without a retreat.

Sunday morning as we built a little breakfast fire in the schoolhouse yard a voice called, "Come on in to breakfast!" And there, leaning on the fence at the back of the yard, was the owner of *The Cellular Universe*. We thanked him, but declined, and presently his wife appeared at the fence with a covered dish of griddle cakes, homemade sausage, and a square of chocolate cake. The man leaned over the fence and said: "Say, do you reckon that book is so?" To save Peter embarrassment I replied that I considered it a dangerous book, because while I was reading it I could n't help but believe it.

"Well," said the old man, "I 'm not afraid to believe anything that seems so to me."

"Hurrah for you!" cried Peter. "Perhaps I 'd believe it if I could understand it. Anyway, it 's worth the money, is n't it?" he asked uneasily.

"Yes, it is," answered the man. "I 'll work on it this winter."

We went to church. We had never attended a valley church. A very old and feeble man preached courageously on "Old things are passed away," and spent half an hour on the inadvisability of burnt sacrifice and other personal matters concerning the Jews. The sermon was convincing, but the dear old man read from notes, and it was a relief when the organ gasped a prelude and four men sang, — I quote the refrain from memory, —

"I think I see my mother floating there,
  Around the hills of glory with the angels fair;
  Floating, floating, I see my mother there."

This somewhat disconcerting picture was relieved by the beautiful voice of the bass. Utterly without self-consciousness, he gazed through the open door to the blue hills beyond, and his voice rolled out, sonorous, sweet, true, expressive. There was, to him, nothing incongruous in the vision of his mother floating there just as he remembered her, with the addition of wings. Nor was there to me while his rich voice boomed out the refrain. We waited to speak to him after the service. He was the village carpenter. A simple man, and, I feel sure, as fine and as true as his voice.

Monday morning the ponderous banker with the soft drawl and shrewd eyes gave us the money, and I humbly asked Peter to carry it. I reminded him that traveler's checks had always brought me misfortune. For once, when we were passing through a Southern city, I looked up from lunch on the gallery of our apartment into two gleaming pistols, and looked down at two armed policemen in the yard below. All because one is expected, absurdly enough, to sign one's name as well in a mood of depression as when one happens to be enjoying a moment of ease and quiet nerves! The law seems rather an inhuman, unreasonable thing. But I have a criminal record, having once before been arrested for refusing to pay an outrageous city license on a car of apples I had raised. These cases were settled in my favor at once; and never, in the clutches of the law, have I had such a feeling of utter helplessness as at the window of the bank in this valley town.

I was feverishly anxious to climb the mountain and forget the marts of men. For to one of us this journey meant not only an escape from the world, but a last good-bye to earth. Soon, we thought, one of us must greet the summer dawns and watch the winter stars alone. And while the devout believe in the communion of saints, and admit, perhaps, the companionship of spirits quick or dead, yet no spirit may put his face against the rough bark of a tree and,

listening for its heartbeat, say, "I too, brother!"
Nor may he break the smooth surface of blue water
where long ago an Indian cooled his bronzed breast,
or dappled fawns drank timidly, and say, "I too pass
this way, with our sister the rain and our brother the
wind." Dust to dust. No more the dear close kinship with the earth, whatever star the eye of faith
may discern in the impenetrable darkness beyond.

"Now," said Peter, gently but firmly, "we are
compelled to walk down the valley road. There is
absolutely no way over the mountain here."

It was a blow. For though this fertile valley
would have brought joy to the heart of a farmer, the
trees were all cut down for fields, and no bird sang.
Only a meadow lark on a rail fence sang his song
"twice over," and no impudent mocking bird
derided. But the insects droned through the "lazy
jack," as the negroes call the drifting heat waves;
and the sun blazed down on the unshaded way.
The road was being repaired, and we met motor cars
in deepest grief, while the spirited horses of the valley
shied always at Sis and rendered us unpopular on the
road.

Late in the afternoon we came upon a little feudal
valley where a great house bullied the surrounding
tenant cottages. Suddenly a splendid race horse
bore down upon us. Our inoffensive Sisyphus
appeared to him as a monster of such frightful mien
that we expected to see his rider, a boy of twelve
perhaps, thrown at our feet. But we did not know

Richard then! When he was safely past us and we had sighed relief, there was a thunder of hoofs and the struggle began once more. Again and again the boy forced the terrified animal past the cart, until at last the horse stood trembling and snorting beside us. Four great black eyes blazed at us alike. Then the boy in the elegant riding breeches and billowing silk shirt suddenly patted the arched neck, and they were off without a word.

The day was gray now and sullen clouds loomed in the west, so we pushed Sis under a tall oak in a vacant lot between two small houses, one of which seemed unoccupied, and began hurriedly to make camp. "Hi there!" called a voice, and the horse took the ditch before the lot with a splendid jump. "It 's going to rain in a minute like the very devil!" cried the boy in a curious voice starting in a gruff bass and ending in a muted tenor. "Go into that empty house at the left. I 'll get the key." He dashed to the house at the right, and called, "Hi! Mr. Bell! Bring out the key to Paw's house!" An old man appeared with the key. The boy tied his horse to the fence, and we followed them into the house — un-furnished, but with a welcoming fireplace. "No chairs," said the boy, and, running back to Mr. Bell's house, he brought over two chairs. Then he mounted his horse and rode away.

"Who is that remarkable person?" I asked.

"That 's Richard. Richard Winstone. His paw owns about everything in the valley, and he does just what he pleases. His paw can't do anything with him. He's the only boy. His sister's just home from boarding school and he pesters the life out of her. Don't worry. It'll be all right — your stopping here. Lord! The old man'd be glad if that's the worst he'd do! He'll be back right away."

And he was; appearing on foot, and bearing two generous slices of ham and a segment of loaf cake. "Richard," said Mr. Bell, "you stole that ham and cake! You'll get these folks in trouble. Now don't take nothing from nobody else."

"I did n't steal 'em. I got 'em at home. Mister, can you play that violin?"

It rained. We built a fire in the fireplace, sat on real chairs, and dined sumptuously. As Peter lighted a luxurious tailor-made cigarette, I saw the green shutters move, and a decapitated fowl fell in the middle of the floor. A gruff voice called, "For breakfast!" Peter rushed to the window and cried, "Richard, you really must not go on like this! You'll get us in bad in the village!"

"No, I'll not!" cried the sweet tenor. "That pullet was n't ours. I got it at Miller's. He owes Paw anyway. I'll be back with some folks to hear you play the violin."

He returned with three men and a boy, who appeared rather apologetic. But not Richard. As I played he sat on the floor in his fine gray breeches and beat time on the hearth with the poker.

He was satisfied with the performance, for he said to the audience, "Now there's Dorothy. She's been squeaking away on her violin — taking lessons ever since I was a kid, and you know the lonesome stuff she pulls out!"

During our stay of two rainy days I fancy Richard ate and slept little. We snatched what we could. For when he was not raiding the village for supplies for us he was sitting before the fire on the floor, asking eager questions about the world outside. In vain did his father send men with messages telling him to return home at once. Richard would answer amiably, "Tell Paw I'll be on directly." And once he said, "You go tell Paw he's got these folks all wrong. You tell Dorothy to come over and hear this woman play on the violin. She might learn something. You tell Paw these folks are all right. They are not gypsies."

Fearing Richard would accompany us, on the morning of the third day we stole away at dawn, leaving a note of thanks for many favors. But at our noon camp there came the sound of galloping hoofs, and there was Richard with a loaf of homemade bread and a whole cake. He lunched with us, delighted with our oven dug in the ground, where we had baked an apple pie, covering it with the iron lid we carried. As he leaned against a tree with a lighted cigarette, there was the sound of wheels. "That's Paw," he said resignedly. An irate voice called, "Richard, you get on your horse and come home. This minute, sir!"

"Which road are you going to take?" asked
Richard, as he mounted his horse. "Maybe I 'll be
back to-morrow."

We watched him ride away behind the cart, in
which his father slumped wearily. From the rear
he gently lifted a white flour sack which appeared
to be heavy, and, leaning from his horse, softly
deposited it in the road. Then he made a time-
honored gesture with his thumb toward his father,
waved his velvet cap, and pointed to the sack with
his riding whip. Peter wanted to rush after the cart
and call. But why get Richard in trouble at this last
moment? So I walked down the road and found
half a bushel of rare peaches with which no doubt
some tenant had presented his father on the way.
Dear, lawless, generous Richard of the lion's heart!
He told us he was to be sent away to school in the fall.
Upon what school he descended, and which came
out on top, we never learned. "Feudalism," said
Peter, "has its points." Weeks later, at a mountain
post office, we received a marked copy of a little
county paper.

Some of the nicest folks ever in this valley camped here
this week. And the lady could play the violin better than
some folks who took lessons for five years. Come again!

"Richard's fine Italian hand," I said. "His last
gesture of defiance."

"I wish," said Peter, "I could have seen him defy-
ing that editor!"

Still we must pursue the valley road. And at sunset we camped in a grove beside a little church. Suddenly from the church came the sound of most exhilarating jazz. I peeped in at the open door. Two young men were smoking cigarettes; one lolled in the pulpit chair, and one thumped joyously on the tin-pan piano. "Come in!" called the youth in the pulpit. Though I confess that I was shocked at this surprising irreverence, I sat down to rest and to listen; and after a while complimented the youth at the piano on the quality of his jazz.

"Oh, I just play by ear," he said modestly. "I can only play in the black keys."

"Some players think that difficult," I said.

"Can you play?"

"Only a little."

The youth in the pulpit had already gone out, and was curiously watching Peter make camp. I gazed away to the mountains through the open door, and rather ungraciously played Mendelssohn, and drifted into scraps of Beethoven, as befitting a church.

I said, "I fear I can't play anything in a church that you will care for." I was rewarded for my priggishness. "Ho," said the youth, "music is music! What has a church to do with it?"

It was one of those haunted summer nights when the world suddenly blanches under a bright moon and as suddenly vanishes under a flying cloud. We sat before the tent in silence, when the two young men of the church appeared and asked us to go in a car up the mountain to a house where there was a piano, and play the violin. We declined. They insisted. But we had no desire to career up a dangerous mountain road in the night, with two unknown men, to an unknown destination — probably a moonshine party. They went away, visibly disappointed; and presently one returned alone, and sat quietly beside us. "You see," he said, "I thought maybe you-all might think we wanted you to go to some low-down party up the mountain. These people we want you to go play for are nice folks. Valley folks. They went to live up on the mountain because Roy — he was my buddy in the war — was sick. Could n't breathe good in the valley. He 's been wounded — in the face — and he 's been gassed. He can't live much longer. His mother lives up there alone with him. She 's seventy-five and she plays the piano fine. I telephoned about you-all, and they want you to come mighty bad. You see, Roy was going to marry Judge Weir's girl in the valley here, and he would n't marry her after he was gassed — and he don't look nice now — his face is all shot up. But she wanted to marry him. They are mighty lonesome nights up the mountain."

Already I was taking my heavy coat from Sis, and Peter was assisting the youth in pushing the cart into the church and locking the door. But I insisted that John come with us. If we were to be kidnaped we should at least all die together.

"Is it far?" asked Peter, as we glided down the

valley road. "It's the first road up the mountain," the driver answered ambiguously. After what seemed a long drive, we turned to the left and ascended the mountain. The moon would suddenly light some deep gorge over which we seemed to hang suspended. Around hairpin curves and over great rocks we rushed. We splashed through unseen waters, and skidded on sandy hills. On and on with these two reckless youths who smoked and played jazz in a church, and who told a preposterous romantic tale to lure us here. I clutched John tightly, pulled my coat about me in the chill air, and resolved to sell my life dearly. Peter said, "Are you cold?" And one of the youths said that he had a bottle of good liquor, and if I did n't mind taking a drink from the bottle it would warm me. I did n't mind. If it were knock-out drops the pangs of dissolution would be eased; and presently when the moon came out I could look down a precipice calmly.

At last we stopped, and to my relief a man appeared with a flash light and conducted us across a yard into a great, bare, dimly lighted hall where a grandfather's clock ticked, and on into a well-furnished living room where, before an open fire, stood a little, gray, black-eyed, birdlike old lady in black silk. At first I was cold with fright, for fear I could not understand the speech of this fair-haired, tall youth who had been so handsome, and who yet lived on a while in his marred beauty. But his friends unobtrusively helped me to understand him.

His mother played a nice accompaniment for simple airs, the youth of the five flats pounded out enticing jazz, and Peter told his funniest stories. After a while our hostess tinkled old-fashioned polkas and mazurkas, and we sang, — not war songs, not a word of the war, — and we were all merry together.

Then Roy asked me if I would play at the telephone in the hall. Radios were slow to penetrate the mountains, and he wanted a friend in the valley to hear. He called someone, and I followed him into the hall. "Can you play 'Good-bye, Summer'?" he asked. "She likes that song." And as my fingers searched the strings for the familiar air he leaned his yellow head against the wall, where the light fell from the open door, and covered his disfigured face with his hands. As the old clock ticked away his life — and mine — I had a curious feeling that neither of us was there, on the mountain, in the shadowy hall — that only the broken shell of the youth was there against the wall, and that he himself walked proudly down the valley road with another, and that I myself was but an echo of the night through the gulf that divided these lovers. And always, as I recall that moment, I have a strange feeling that I left something of myself there on the lonely mountain. Or a feeling that I was not I, but a voice calling over and over again, "Good-bye! Good-bye, Summer!"

I finished, and left the boy leaning against the wall, with his scarred face in his hands.

Presently I heard him at the telephone, and after a

while he appeared from another room with a tray bearing a great bowl of eggnog and little old-fashioned seed cakes, and he served us with feverish gayety. The little old lady and Peter danced while I played a waltz; and the other lad and I fox-trotted to hilarious jazz. Then Roy said, "It's late and cold, and you are not going down the mountain to-night. You are going to stay here, and we'll have fried chicken and waffles and honey for breakfast!" But the gay little lady was weary now, and her hand trembled on the railing as she climbed the stairs before me to show me the room with its dainty curtains and hooked rugs. As she said good-night she murmured, "I want to thank you for coming to cheer my boy. He's lonely. And I'm seventy-five, and he's all I have. He'll not be here much longer." The white head raised itself proudly. "But I'm not afraid."

What had I to offer that dauntless spirit?

At breakfast we were gay. And there were yellow roses on snowy linen, and a single waxen-white rose at my plate.

On the way down the mountain the driver said, "Jim, we ought to come up oftener to see Roy. Some day he'll go West and we'll feel pretty mean. He's lonesome. Let's bring the girls and come up Sunday. He misses the valley folks."

"Dear kind valley folks!" I cried, patting his shoulder.

"Belated justice," said Peter. And the boy turned surprised young eyes upon us.

IX

CLEANIN' UP THE COUNTY

"THAR ain't no spring on this-hyar road. But effen you-all is thirsty, thar's a big spring th'ough the timber ter the left. Hain't no path ter hit, ye might say, but hit won't mis-putt me none to stanter a ways 'ith you-all."

John, with the wisdom of dogs, gave the bearded mountaineer one long look, and, discrediting the story of a spring, disappeared toward a fringe of willows bordering the distant river.

We were thirsty and tired, and we "stantered" what seemed a long way. Suddenly the man, with no preamble, said, "I reckon I'll jist turn back now." And he set off down the hill. We gazed at each other in astonishment.

"Hi there!" called Peter. "Where's the spring?"

"Mister, jist kim down hyar a minute, an' I 'll tell ye sumpen."

I offered Peter the rifle I carried, but he refused it, and walked back down the hill. I followed him with an anxious eye, my finger on the trigger of the gun. For all day we had seen fresh boughs in the road pointing to dim paths that led to "a snort o' liquor." But more than hidden stills I feared the motor cars — not much smaller than the desolate cabins before which they stood. For the manufacture of moonshine is an old, dignified, established business in the mountains, but the get-rich-quick distributors are often reckless "furriners," and their cars sometimes carry intoxicated parvenus.

After what seemed a long time, Peter climbed the hill, pushed Sisyphus into the shade of a sweet gum tree, and carefully rolled a cigarette. I whistled for John and waited.

"The man," said Peter, "tells me that you are a mighty likely womern."

"Indeed! He might have blurted that out before me. I should n't have cared. Is that what he called you back to tell you?"

"I gathered as much. He advised us to 'go on a leetle furder, camp fur the night, and turn back at sunup.' We are almost at the county line, and they 're 'cleanin' up' the next county. Now just how bright is the face of danger to you this afternoon?"

"Radiant, as always. Cleanin' up a county should n't dim it."

"It 's this. They are chasing out the moonshiners in dead earnest in the next county, and the moonshiners are doubly ferocious and suspicious of informers. He says that the whole county is given over to religious revivals. 'Thar hain't nobody kin git a snort o' liquor, exceptin' they take Communion at church, 'ithout gittin' shot at. Both sides is pow'ful het up, an' effen they wuz ter git hit inter thar haids you-all wuz informers, they might take a crack at you-all frum behint a rock afore they knowed better. They is Gawddlemighty keerful jest now, fur ivery other man in the county is a deppity sheriff. An' that-air womern o' yourn a-pintin' a gun at me up ther hill is a pow'ful likely womern to run a chancet o' bein' a widder womern.'"

"The man's judgment is sound. Anyone can see that! But back trails are not thrilling. Let 's go on. It 's only one night before we get to the village. Nothing can happen in one night."

"It would n't take longer than one night to shoot a man. But it 's coming on to rain, and the tent is leaking. We can get beeswax and oil to paint it in the village. We can reach Avola to-morrow afternoon and go in a safe camp near the town — safe unless they take us for evolutionists."

"Oh, we look like fundamentalists. We could pass anywhere now."

John came, a streak of white through the green field, and we set out at a rapid pace for the church, where the mountaineer had said there was "a good well o' water; an' 'bout half a quarter furder a store kep' by a furriner frum Texas."

"And now," said· Peter, "effen inybody says ter us, 'Jist move on an' don't look back,' we 're jist ter move on. An' effen inybody stanters with us kinder offen the road, we 're not ter be curious-like, but jist talk pleasant-like that we is takin' a tower fur the womern's health."

"Oh, we always do that!"

It was twilight when we came to a small frame church crouched in a sallow, dank hollow, surrounded with pines. But the pump was painted a cheerful pink, and the water was delicious. The doors were locked, and I peered through an open window at the back. "Why, it is a schoolhouse! There is a little blackboard. But there 's a pulpit, and a Bible."

Suddenly there came a few great drops of rain, and the thirsty earth answered at once with rich perfume.

"The lantern is empty!" cried Peter. "I 'll run up to that store for kerosene. Back in a minute."

I looked about for a place to trench for our leaking tent. We often slept in schoolhouses; but a church — that is different. Schoolhouses in the mountains are used for anything other than school. In a summer's wandering we had found but one schoolhouse functioning properly. But that one rewarded us. It was the first week of school, and the tall, erect young mountaineer who was the teacher apologized for lack of order. Order! Why, the petrified children sat on hard benches like little statues.

"It is extremely difficult to maintain order at first in a strange settlemint," said the teacher carefully. "But after I whoop a few of the larger pupils several times they settle down. Hit 's — it 's a new neighborhood to me."

We sat on the front bench and watched a little boy, with hair so white it had a cast of blue, as he glowered down at the primer on the teacher's knee.

"Now this is *A*," said the teacher. "Look at it good."

The boy backed away, and looked up scowling. "How do ye know hit 's *A*?" he asked contemptuously.

"Because hit 's right thar in the book" — falling into the vernacular from the shock. The boy scratched his brown leg with a bare foot. Then, as if considering it too trifling a matter for contention, he said, "Huh! All right, hit 's *A*."

As we left, Peter asked the boy his name, which was Elmer Bond, and slipped him a quarter. He vows that child is destined to wipe out fundamentalism in his state.

The rain delayed. I prepared the "jambalaya" and set it on the camp fire I had built. It makes a comforting supper on rainy nights — that, with cookies bought from a village housewife, and tea. For "tea is the boy for the woods."

Peter ran down the hill with the lighted lantern, and we hurried to cut pine boughs for a bed — though, unless one has learned the art of making a

pine-bough bed, there is need for a chiropractor by
midnight.

"We'll sleep in the schoolhouse," said Peter.

"The church," I corrected. "I hope no one will
see our light. They may know nothing of sanctuary."

As the door was locked, Peter threw in a great
armful of boughs through the window, and I started
to cast in my smaller contribution. There was a
crash, the sound of an overturned bench, and the
front door slammed.

Peter dragged me back out of the light of the fire
and whispered, "Be quiet! It's that fellow from
the store, spying. He hasn't any stock in the store.
It's a bootlegging joint."

Presently from the wood across the road from the
church sounded "Halloo! Halloo!" Peter, from
behind a tree, answered with another halloo, and
around the church strode the Texas "furriner" and
stood before the fire. He was tall and rangy, and his
moustaches were fierce and wide. His flannel shirt
gleamed red in the firelight, and there was a pistol
in the holster at his belt. He carried a jug. "Say,
stranger, why n't you answer? I ben a-hollerin',
fur I couldn't locate yore camp. Hyar's the key ter
the church. It's goin' ter rain like hell and blazes.
Better sleep thar. I reckon you're jist driftin' and
you'll move on ter-morrow. And hyar's a jug o'
milk I thought yore womern might like."

He unlocked the door, but refused to enter with us.

"No, it 's goin' ter rain cats and dogs and nigger babies. So long."

I could n't keep the quaver from my voice. "He was listening inside the church! If we had said the wrong thing I might be here alone now."

"Oh, I guess not," said Peter, but without conviction.

We pushed Sisyphus into the church, and supper was served in grand style on a desk. The milk the Texan had brought us was, of course, buttermilk. Sweet milk is so called, and is churned sweet. Buttermilk is a beverage. It looked delicious, but with my first taste I set down the cup. "Taste it! Is he trying to poison us?" Peter tasted the milk from my cup, and looked serious. He poured himself another cup, and grinned. "I think," he said, "the next county is on our nerves. I 'm afraid I left the soap in your cup at noon."

It was cool, and the rain drummed softly on the shingles, and the pine-bough bed was delightfully fragrant. John curled up at the foot, and I drew the blanket about me in the perfect peace that comes from an all-day tramp on the open road. Peter took the Bible from the pulpit and said, "We may as well bone up for the next county; I 'll read you to sleep."

There is no sleep, at least to me, so deep or so sweet as that into which we sink while a familiar voice reads from a book, well written, but not so eloquent that it wakes the mind to wonder, or the heart to ecstasy. For undirected thoughts will seek dark paths that lead away from the sea of sleep, and music with its melody and rhythm lulls the mind, but the soul stirs uneasily and at the mystery of beauty wakes to ancient pain; and too often the beating, baffled wings of prayer pursue us, spent and bewildered, to the very shore of sleep.

Peter chose to read from the Psalms. But who could sleep while David bares his great human heart to God!

Long ago, someone — was it well-loved Peter Ibbetson? — taught me to cry "Crac" to the reveille of "Cric" which the patient reader calls to find if I am still awake. And what a rare pleasure to turn back a moment from the engulfing wave of sleep and to float away again on its deep calm tide.

"Peter," I say apologetically, "would you mind changing the subject?"

He switches to Revelation. But outlandish horned beasts emerge from the shadows, and Death on the pale horse bears down upon me, and all the gigantic pageantry of Revelation thunders past.

"Crac!" I cry desperately, sitting up wide-awake.

Peter laughs, and in a low monotonous voice, which blends with the gentle drumming of the rain on the roof, reads a page of "begats" — and I know no more till the morning sun streams through the dusty windows of the church.

We stopped at the store to return the jug, and to thank the Texan for our night's shelter.

"Stranger," he said, "sence you appear to be driftin' to Avoly, it 'd better your hand, I believe, to take the trail to the left and cut off some miles. By the help and assistance o' good luck and some sense you 'll come out on top of the mountain whar the road leads down to the dad-gasted town that 'd give any growed-up man the popeyed willies jist to look down on!"

Remembering the warning of the friendly mountaineer, we meekly took the trail to the left. With the aid of our pocket compass and the moss on the north side of the trees, we wandered north over great boulders and through small canyons, tying a rope to John's chain and hauling long-suffering Sis up and down precipices by main force.

"That bootlegger," said Peter, "must have had his lingering doubts that we might report stills to the next county."

There was lunch and a long rest on the summit of the mountain, and the setting sun was flinging rosy fleece over a sea of faintest green when we came to the outskirts of the village. A man who was sweeping out a church said, "'Bout half a quarter back o' the church thar 's a good campin' spot whar thar 's good water in the crick." He called after us, "Thar 's a big meetin' goin' on hyar! Kim over ter-night! We 're cleanin' up the whole consarned county!"

It was an ideal spot for a camp. A low, rounded hill crowned with tall pines. Below ran a clear stream where great symmetrical sweet gums guarded the blossoming laurel. We spread our blankets beneath the haughty pines that stared down in silent scorn upon the deciduous trees that pay court to rivers and when winter comes stand stark and humiliated. For in the veins of the Southern pine runs liquid fire.

Suddenly the full moon is here, and the river and the moon sing together. For while by day the streams murmur, it is only at night that the waters wake and sing.

We lay weary, but not exhausted, on our bed of pine needles, and presently from the church came the sound of voices singing "Onward, Christian soldiers! Marching as to war." There was a certain pathos in the thought that here were people calling on their deepest instincts to root out a one-time innocent custom dear to them through generations, to prove their allegiance to a law more honored in the breach than in the observance over all America. Then we fell asleep to the pleasant drone of the "Sweet By and By."

The following morning we left John to guard camp, and carried the wheel of Sisyphus to the village for repairs. Before the combined blacksmith's shop and garage stood a young but dissipated-looking automobile surrounded by a small group of men. Peter took the wheel inside to the blacksmith, and I listened to the animated conversation of the men about the car.

"How you stand on the cow, Ramsey?" asked an old mountaineer. "I 'm whole hawg or nothin' fur the *man*. Hain't no use bein' a plumb fool effen a man *is* a Christian."

Ramsey answered: "Hit's a case o' a man perviden fur his own family, which the Bible says a man orter do first!"

"Wal," said the first speaker, "hit air a cur'ous thing that the onliest folks that object ter the cow deal is the Holy Rollers and one infi-*del*. Never knowed 'em to agree afore!"

"Hit's my opinion," said another, "thet Brother Martin hes bit off more 'n he kin chaw this time — in regards to cows. Hit air outen his line! A preacher better let business alone, and stan' squar' on preachin' thet Jesus Christ 's the Son o' God!"

"Shucks!" said the first speaker. "I verbody in the world knows Jesus Christ's the Son o' God. Thar hain't no use *re*-peatin' hit all the time. Brother Martin is aimin' at makin' practical Christians."

"All I kin say, he 's stirred up Avoly and this settlemint. An' whichiver way he decides hit Sunday mornin' thar 's goin' ter be argumints and hard feelin's. I believe in stickin' ter the Gospel. A feller kin work out his own practical experience."

I was tremendously interested, and felt it was unfortunate that Peter should appear from the shop just then and we should have to hurry on to the store for beeswax and linseed oil to paint our tent while the sun shone.

Two women leaned over a gate talking together. "I wusht to the Lord thet cow 'd niver ben borned!" cried one. "Pappy don't talk o' nothin' else and hain't hauled up a stick o' timber sence last Sunday. I ben pickin' splinter offen the back fence fur firewood fur cookin' iver sence that air pesky cow-trouble was turned loose on us!"

Farther on an old man, evidently deaf, put his hand to his ear and called to a young fellow working in his garden, "How ye standin' on the cow, Jim?"

"'Pears lak hit seems thet I jist cain't make up my mind noways!" yelled the young man, frowning, and stopping to lean on his hoe. "But I got twell ter-morrow mornin'. Maybe I 'll get enlightenmint afore mornin'."

"Peter," said I, "have we by any chance wandered into India? Why, a sacred cow is the one topic of conversation here! Try to find out what it 's all about."

There were two stores, but we selected the one that held the post office. For we had learned that here, beside the ubiquitous checkerboard behind the stove, usually sat the wisdom club of the village. Peter bought his material for painting the tent, and then selected himself an empty nail keg with the group behind the stove. Women are debarred from the wisdom club. The two vital questions discussed are sex and religion. And a mountain man considers a woman sufficiently endowed by nature and by God with both. Hers not to reason why, hers but to do and die.

So I waited in the front of the store, and bought a dozen eggs from a tall, sad woman, who took off her blue sunbonnet and fanned herself wearily.

"Have you walked far ?" I asked.

"Not ter say fur," she replied in her thin, monotonous voice. "A leetle better 'n two mile. But I hain't no 'count. I jist got over the flus, an' I got a enlarged melt. Hit runs up an' down in my side. Jist putt yore hand thar an' feel hit."

I hastily asked her if she had consulted a physician.

"Yeah. I thought hit war a chill-cake in my side, but I wint ter thet doc over in Springdale — thet fat doc — I disremember his name. He 'lowed hit war high blood pressure a-movin' hit up an' down thetaway. But I hain't murch use fur thim newfangled docs. Jist afore I kim down 'ith the flus, I stayed 'ith Arreny Reed, — she thet wuz Arreny Wear, ye know, — an' whin the baby kim thet fat doc frum Springdale wuz thar. She had the peartest leetle boy ye iver see. But thet doc said thar war another; an' hit could n't be borned nohow. Arreny kep' beggin' fur her snuff, an' thet fool doc would n't let me give hit to her. I slipped out an' got a fresh althy stick, but he cotched me afore I could dip hit inter the snuff can an' slip hit to Arreny. Finally the doc sets down by the haid o' the baid an' says, pow'ful solemn, 'Wal, Miss Reed, I done all I kin. We 'll hafter sind ter Springdale fur instermints. I 'll give you some easin' medicine now.'

"Arreny hollers, 'You gimme my snuff! I don't want none o' yer easin' medicine! Gimme my snuff!' 'Fore the doc kin say inything, I grabs the snuff can an' hands hit to Arreny. Her hand is trimblin', an' afore she gits hit under her lip hit scatters on the quilt; an' Arreny begins ter sneeze, an' tother wuz borned to oncet! Peartest leetle gal ye iver see! Thim docs don't know murch nowadays."

I tried, hopelessly, to give the woman some idea of diet. But well I knew that all the good green food from her garden must be cooked with pork "afore hit's fitten fur humans." Even lettuce is never eaten without "bein' wilted 'ith ham grease." But I bought the three shriveled oranges displayed in the show case. The woman accepted them reluctantly and gave me no thanks, but her eyes shone.

Peter appeared, and as we set out I asked if he had learned anything regarding the sacred cow of the village. "The city preacher from Springdale," he said, "put a question to Avola at the church last Sunday. He is to speak on the question to-morrow morning. We'll go to church. He asked them to think on the question, but I suppose he did n't know they would think of nothing else. A man had a cow to sell which he had priced at forty dollars. Some mountain cow, I'd say! A stranger moves in who belongs to the same church as the man with the cow, and wishes to buy it. The owner, who knows that the stranger comes from afar, — a better country,

where cows are cows, — sells him the cow for fifty
dollars. Was the man justified in raising the price
on his Christian brother? The village is divided
against itself, and as the preacher is running for the
legislature his friends are uneasy, for whichever way
he decides it 's bound to lose him some votes. I 'm
wondering just how that preacher will sidestep."

At camp we hurriedly prepared to paint the tent.
As I dipped my brush in the hot mixture, I looked up
and whispered, "A visitor."

Slowly down the hill walked a very tall, deep-
chested man, who carried a shotgun.

"I seen you-all at Perry's store," he said, seating
himself under a pine, "an' I jist 'lowed I 'd stanter
over an' see how you-all wuz comin' on."

We explained that it was necessary to go on with
our work, and apologized. He turned great gentle
blue eyes upon me and said in a voice of velvet:
"I 'm the constable o' Avoly. I seed Billy Godbehere a-sneakin' th'ough thet fenced-in field across the
road frum you-all's tint. The deppity sheriff 's got
Billy's cow shet in thar. Hit hain't rightly none o'
my business, but the sheriff 's a-lookin' fur Billy Godbehere, an' hit would n't surprise me none effen thar
wuz a leetle mite o' a ruckus. Link don't reely aim
ter shoot Billy, I reckon. Hit 's likely, though, he 'll
shoot eround 'nuff ter putt the fear o' God in Billy."

"What," said Peter, rolling Billy Godbehere's
name delightedly under his tongue, "has Billy
Godbehere done?"

"He air lettin' the boys hev liquor. I tole Billy ter stop hit whin we all begin cleanin' up the county. He don't 'pear ter take hit serious a-tall. Thet's Billy a-runnin' th'ough the field now," he drawled. "An' hyar kims Link after him lickety-split! I reckon you-all better pick out a tree ter git behint."

He selected his own tree with surprising agility for so large a man, and we chose adjacent trees. Peering around my tree, I saw across the lane in the fenced field a tall man running zigzag from one persimmon clump to another, while a short, square-set man pursued him, waving a gun and yelling, "Hold up, Billy! I aim ter shoot!" But the tall man ran on, dodging and doubling, and evidently trying to reach the fence.

Suddenly a bullet whined through the boughs above us. The constable turned edgeways to his tree and stood as still and as erect as an Indian. Another bullet sang high above us, and the spectacle was lost to me until I heard a great shouting and a motor rattled down the lane from the direction of the town. It stopped for a second; the tall man, with a mighty leap, cleared the fence and fell into the car, which vanished down the road. That car, even in its own class, was no doubt socially extinct, but it cleared the river in one jump and tore up the hill on the other side with amazing speed.

The short man climbed the fence, slowly crossed the lane, and sank at the foot of the constable's tree. Wiping the sweat from his face with his sleeve, he

gasped, "Now wuz n't thet a sight on airth how Billy
Godbehere got erway! I see Lee Ramsey's car settin' afore the shop, an' I knowed the Ramseys and
Godbeheres is kin. But Lee 'lowed the car wuz
plumb busted. Said he'd hafter haul hit inter
Springdale fur a new amateur, an' sumpen inside
needed a assanine torch. I might a knowed Lee
lied! Say, Joe, why n't ye kim over 'n' holp?
'Stid er settin' hyar on yer hunkies watchin' Billy git
erway!"

"Wal," drawled the constable in his gentle voice,
"fust place, I wuz n't settin' on no hunkies whilst you
wuz a-shootin' plumb at these strangers — an' one a
womern, too. I hain't no deppity sheriff. I'm a
constable, pyore an' simple. I got troubles enough
'ith my court. I don't ricollict o' hyarin' o' yore
holpin' me none in the argumints round Piney Hill
Church when I wuz follerin' up my sorter mixed-up
settlin' o' law an' Christianity at one lick."

"I 'low thet wuz different," said the sheriff. "Hit
wuz thet mixed up hit 'd take a lawyer an' a preacher
ter settle hit."

"I jist puzzled th'ough hit rightly, effen hit did
start some argumint. I 'll leave hit ter this stranger.
Hit war thisaway."

The little sheriff bit off a comforting chew of
tobacco, and Peter rolled a cigarette.

"Jeff Ross, he driv up ter ther meetin' at Piney
Hill Church one night frum sellin' a wagonload o'
watermelons an' mushmelons at Springdale, an' he lit

right out fur the mourners' bench an' claimed he got religion right off. He smelt strong o' liquor an' pranced round onseemly, an' the young folks on the back seat sniggered. Next mornin' I up an' fined him five dollars — as a constable, o' course. But whin Jeff Ross he kim ter church thet night an' claimed he kim th'ough an' wuz saved the night afore, I remitted his fine — as a Christian, o' course. Hit ain't fur me ter say thet Jeff did n't git shed o' his sins thet night whin he wuz tight. I don't noways aim ter shorten ther Sperrit's power, but I 'lows Gawddlemighty Hisself might find hit handier ter convart a skunk lak Jeff Ross whin he 's sorter softened up an' out er hisself. An' I 'm hyar to say a man hed better git religion whin he kin — drunk er sober. Thar 's a heap o' argumints 'bout how I handled thet case round erbout ther settlemint, but I claim I done right twicet!"

"My opinion," said Peter judicially, "is that you showed a great deal of wisdom, and a cold, correct nerve. You done right twicet."

"Ter-morrow is Sunday," said the constable softly, "an' thar 's a big baptizin' in the river back o' my place. You-all kin go home 'ith me after meetin' an' go to the baptizin' an' stay all night. Hain't no preachin' Sunday night. I 'll kim in ther big wagon an' haul you-all's little contraption erlong. Your womern 'pears to like dogs. I want you-all ter see my houn's. I ben offered more 'n seventy-five dollars fur ole Tod."

I exchanged a glance with Peter and accepted the
invitation.   It was on our road to Springdale, and I
liked the constable, and I wanted to see Tod.

The next morning we tied John to the wheel of
Sisyphus and left the cart near an open window of the
crowded church.   Peter sat with the men at the
right, and I with the meek sisters at the left.   The
portly preacher from Springdale looked over the
faces in his congregation with shrewd, kindly eyes.
He read for the morning lesson the seventh chapter of
Saint Matthew, and took his text from the first verse :
"Judge not, that ye be not judged " The sermon
was simple, tolerant, and even fervent.   And his
impressive voice ended solemnly : "With what
measure ye mete, it shall be measured to you again."

Then suddenly he stepped down from the little
platform and with a friendly smile addressed us.
"Here speaks the politician, not the preacher," I
thought.

But the frozen Sabbath faces in the congregation
never changed by the flicker of an eyelash, though
each man knew the question of the day was now
before the house.   Only Peter smiled delightedly at
the masterly manner in which the candidate for the
legislature sidestepped.

For we must first of all learn charity.   Who can
read the heart of a man who has a cow to sell ?   God
alone can do that.   The question he had propounded
each man must answer for himself according to the
dictates of his own conscience, but bearing in mind

his own limitations and the necessity for charity. Beware of judgment. The day the man offered the cow for forty dollars he may have been in financial distress, and, hoping for a quick sale, put too low a price on the cow. He may the next day have been offered more for cream and butter, thus enhancing the cow's value. His children may have been so attached to this particular cow that they must be pacified by an extra ten dollars. His wife may have held an interest in the cow which the man had forgotten the day before. Who are we to judge a man selling a cow? Is a merchant unjust that his prices fluctuate with the market? The price of cows may have risen overnight.

Solemnly and impressively he closed with the warning words: "Judge not, that ye be not judged."

We all sang "Scatter Seeds of Kindness," and arose to receive the benediction. Peter afterward declared that the appropriate song would have been the one we heard at a Sunday School concert in another county: "You Can't Make a Monkey Out of Me."

Outside there were loud expressions of admiration. Their preacher had "got by"! For the mountaineer, condemned by lack of practice and of opportunity to the harmlessness of the dove, accords generous, if wistful, homage to the man with the wisdom of the serpent.

The little sheriff met us at the door and cried, "I reckon you-all niver seen a slicker talker 'n Brother Martin nowhar a-tall! He knowed he 'd bit off more 'n he could chaw, an' he jist switched the Bible onter us. He 'll git ivery vote in this-hyar settlemint!"

We lifted Sis into the big wagon with the four delighted children. The constable called in his caressing voice to the sleek mules, "Git erlong, now!" and we jolted away down the hot sandy road with John trotting proudly beside us.

X

THE WAY TO NEXT WEDNESDAY

THE mules stopped before a long white-washed log
house, and the constable's four children jumped down
from the jolt wagon. We lifted Sisyphus out, and
the children proudly pushed the cart up the clean-
swept path through the blossoming larkspur and
zinnia.

A wiry red-haired woman in a starched blue calico
dress advanced to meet us.

"Howdy," she said quietly. "Pappy 'lowed as
how you-all 'd kim erlong frum meetin'. I did n't
go. I 'm a Apostolic."

The constable's wife wore that curious air of
serenity which surrounds all Holy Rollers as an
almost palpable aura; and her words carried good
news. For never had we found an Apostolic in the
mountains whose house was not scrupulously clean,

or whose table was not bountifully and neatly set. Tidiness and cleanliness are articles of their faith, though they pride themselves on having neither creed nor church organization.

On the long sunny gallery where the trumpet vine clambered and the honeysuckle bloomed there was set "the visitin' stand table," with its bucket of "drinkin' water," a gourd hanging above the gleaming tin washbasin, and a white towel on its nail. This usually meant that the girl of the house expected a beau. Peter utterly disapproved of this custom; for the fact that a "visitin' stand table" was not on the gallery would proclaim to a Sabbath world that a girl was not popular. But I explained to him that a girl in such a case would hang out the snowiest towel and the shiniest basin. I know *I* should.

On a cushioned bench in the shadiest spot sat an old man evidently just descended from a frieze of the Biblical prophets. This was Grandpap, the constable's father. Like his son, Joe Ross, he was unusually tall, but built more on lines of grace, and his long white hands did not appear toil-worn. He unfolded himself and stood before me, his childlike blue eyes gazing straight into mine. "Howdy," he said, and his eyes roved over Sisyphus. I thought I caught a gleam of amusement — a rare sight. For while a mountain man appreciates his own brand of wit, and may guffaw at a practical joke, the stony melancholy of his face is seldom brightened by a smile.

John immediately recognized Grandpap as belonging to his own world. Some have called our dog an impudent pup, because of his debonair manner and his airs and graces ill befitting, perhaps, his sex or his species. He is an untrained hunter, for we limited his education that he might not prove too attractive to Alabama negroes. But because of his alert air mountain men often tried to trade a good "houn' dawg" for him. Now he pushed Grandpap gently with his paw, and asked him politely to move over. It was months since John had seen a cushion! Grandpap knew dogs. He moved over, but did not offer to pat a strange dog. Instead, he said in a tone not too humbly ingratiating, "Wal, I hyars ye air a murch-traveled purp. Whut ye good fur? Kin ye hunt?"

He spoke quietly, as to an equal, and John answered with a wide, appreciative smile.

I went into "the room" and put my wilted hat on the towering snowy bed. The table was set in the cool dogtrot, and, though there were no screens, there was not a single Apostolic fly!

"Grandpap!" called Mrs. Ross from the open door across the dogtrot. The old man left the gallery and joined her.

"Why n't yer putt on yer good clo'es fur the baptizin', Grandpap? Hit ain't too late yit. Now ye git behint ther baidstid an' putt 'em on," she added coaxingly.

"I did n't reckon, Arreny, as a baptizin' called fur

a man's best. I 'low ther deesciples wore whut they happened ter hev on. I 'm plumb clean — yis'dy wuz Sat'dy. Cou'se, mebby not as clean as a Apostolic man; but purty clean fur a Prisbyterian. An' I shore aimed ter keep thim clo'es fur a dawg fight, er ter be laid erway in, an' make ye perroud o' me oncet, Arreny."

"Grandpap! Hit air plumb weekid ter timpt ther Lord 'ith idle words. Now, jist ter pleasure me, ye git behint ther baidstid an' putt 'em on."

"All right, all right, Arreny. Though hit goes agin my conscience ter pomper yer pride lak thet. An' ye a-aimin' at the Second Blessin'. It 's pow'ful hot ter crouch behint a baidstid jist at dinner time. But I 'll do hit!"

Presently Grandpap joined me on the gallery, looking a trifle uncomfortable but every inch the prophet, with a twinkle lurking in the awful innocence of his eyes.

We dined sumptuously in the dogtrot, and conversed in a most unmountainlike manner. Eating in the mountains is no occasion for levity, and often we have smiled inwardly when our hostess's voice has dropped to lower G and asked solemnly, "Will you-all keer fur some o' thim pickeled beets?"

"This air a gre't day fur ther county," said the constable. "Some o' the Harts an' some o' the Cowdens baptized right tergither. Ther same river a-bearin' ther sins erway. An' thim onnery boys frum Wildcat thet allers fit us — a-turnin' frum thar

evil ways right hyar at Chicken Bristle. We 're
shore clearin' ther county o' liquor an' sin."

"I 'lows, Joe," said Grandpap gently, "thet effen
ye got iny holt over Brother Martin, ye best hev him
putt thim Harts an' Cowdens under ther water fust
thing, an' not wait. I hyar thet sinners in yo'-all's
church hain't shed o' ther sins twell they kims up
outern the water. I dunno myself. But I 'm
thinkin' whilst they is still in the bonds o' sin an'
ineequity they might take a crack at one another.
My pappy war jist a lad whin thim Harts an' Cowdens fust broke out on one another over by Laurel-
hell Holler. I 'low Wanderin' River hit 'll be plumb
choked up 'ith ther sins. Iverbody knowed hit war
Steve Hart thet crippled Jack Cowden, an' hit war
Jack as shot Sam Hart."

"Grandpap," said the constable apologetically,
"'lows er man's sins kin be jist sprinkled erway.
Mebby hisn could. He air lived a pow'ful lengthy
good life."

After dinner we set out at once through the
"deadnin' lot" the short way to the baptizing.
Above a furious little waterfall slept a blue transparent pool reflecting the willows and washing the
white stones in its cool depths. Though we were
cleanin' up the county I was not prepared to see the
entire county gathered here for purification. Such
a throng! Mothers in Israel with glistening white
sunbonnets, solemn men in workday clothes, youths
in Sunday finery, girls and children in pink and gold

and lavender like summer flowers on the river's bank, and babies in arms or asleep on the grass in the shade.

The preacher from Springdale stood, an impressive figure, at the head of a long line of candidates for baptism. We were cleanin' up the county in the only way — saving ourselves one at a time.

Suddenly we began to sing, softly and reverently, "Just As I Am." And the song, stealing on the silence of the summer air, was such a natural thing! The sound seemed to ooze from the landscape. As if the drooping willows, the placid water, the brooding hills, chanted their age-long song of peace and resignation. And we, the heavy-laden, fever-burnt with sense of sin, striving desperately for the spirit of the quiet hills — the peace that passeth understanding.

A gaunt man, with a white, set face, walked down into the pool. The preacher lifted high a sovereign hand. So still it was that we could hear the chuckling of the little waterfall below, and the swish of the reeds by the river. As the man came out of the water and climbed the green bank, I caught a look of rapture on his rugged face. It fell upon his stony countenance like a sudden sun in winter woods.

"Bud Hart," whispered Grandpap. "This 'n a-comin' now air Charlie Cowden."

"Though this pore body lies a-moulderin' in ther tomb,
An' soft winds gintly murmurs o'er hits quiet home,
An' strange sweet flowers in beauty thar will bloom,
Yit — I 'll rest in Heaven."

One after another. Grim-faced men bitten by a late remorse for wild deeds of lawlessness and revenge; adolescents, weighted with youth's sudden, piteous, intolerable sense of sin; weary, toil-worn women anticipating Heaven as rest from incessant labor.

"Thar is rest fur ther weary. Thar is rest fur ther weary. Thar is rest fur ther weary. Thar is rest fur you!"

Always at the lifting of the steady commanding hand we fell silent; and the willows whispered and the little waterfall laughed. And the river, in the old, old rite of initiation and purification, stole away with its burden of regret, remorse, and despair. To these simple people an unquestioned command, blindly obeyed. But I thought, beside this simple and beautiful ceremony, how clumsy and inadequate our confessions, complexes, and transferences to rid the soul of fear and of a sense of sin, when two thousand years ago a spiritual genius went straight to the heart of truth as a homing bird.

John, who had watched all this with interest as a curious game, had been standing quietly by my side. But when, at last, a little girl went under the water, he jerked his chain from my hand and dashed to the rescue. For John was raised on Mobile Bay and knows how far a youngster should go. Grandpap jumped for the chain, missed it, and gallantly put one foot in the water. But I clutched him firmly, and Peter plunged to an unexpected baptism and dragged John to shore.

"I don't 'low as I blame John murch," said Grandpap. "Hit air a big price ter pay fur her leetle sins
— a-mixin' 'em all up 'ith thim Hart an' Cowden
sins! Hit war more 'n her sins kim ter."

Peter flapped past in his wet clothes as Grandpap
and I climbed the path through the deadnin'. "I
hope," said Peter, "that John and I did not queer
the show. It was impressive — that baptizing. I
wonder how much of it was vanity — inflated ego?"

"Why, Peter!" I cried. "Of course vanity,
egoism, hunger, sex, and human nature remained.
But how good to think that fear, regret, remorse, and
despair all drifted away on Wanderin' River to a sea
of forgetfulness."

"I 'lows thim things ye mintion, Peter," said
Grandpap slowly, "is swep' erway in whut Arreny
'lows is ther Second Blessin'. Iver Apostolic hes
got hit, er aims ter git hit. I reckon it 's a low-down
streak in my natur', but I 'm hopin' Arreny won't
git hit twell I 'm dwellin' in my heavenly home.
Whin human natur 's all washed erway, hit 'd kinder
seem lak a drink o' warm branch water in August.
Kim over thisaway and see 'em feed ther houn's."

Lee, the eldest child, a boy of twelve, had hurried
home to feed the hounds their evening "dawg cawn
braid." Oblivious of our approach, he was endeavoring to control the hungry hounds and threatening
them in extremely unapostolic language. The constable and his wife arrived from the baptizing, and
the boy's mother said sadly, "Hit air hard ter raise

up our chillun amongst the ongodly as goes ter ther school." But the constable cried, "Ye heish usin' language, Lee, or I 'll whoop hit outen yer! Hyar, Tod! I ben offered more 'n seventy-five dollars fur this-hyar houn'. Th'ow me a chunk o' cawn braid fur him, Lee. Arreny makes the best dawg cawn braid in ther county!"

"Yeah," said Grandpap. "Iver man in ther county says ther same 'bout his womern, I 'low. We got ter hearten the womern up, er they 'd slay iver houn' in ther kintry."

I murmured polite admiration for Tod, but my words were as hollow as Tod's voice. Of course one must love all dogs, as one must love all men. But hounds are hard to love — lop-eared somnambulists, awakening only to the sound of a horn into maniacal, pursuing demons of chase. But Peter atoned for my hypocrisy with unfeigned admiration for Tod.

After supper we all gathered on the gallery in the moonlight, the air heavy with the scent of "mawk orange" and honeysuckle. Katydids shrilled, and a whippoorwill, seeking his supper in the air, called plaintively, each unfinished cadence ending on the seventh, until I wished that he would shout just one exultant, satisfying tonic over some especially satisfying morsel. The children flitted about on the grass catching fireflies and imprisoning them in bottles. At last the constable called softly, "Come on in, chillun. Turn thim lightnin' bugs loose now, an' come in ter baidtime prayer."

We knelt in the moonlight, our faces in the split-bottom chairs, and the constable abandoned his velvet voice for the long-drawn whine on the fifth of his scale — the tone reserved for addressing the Deity in the mountains. But it was a good prayer, tried and true. We had heard it that morning at church. After an appropriate introduction, the constable continued with a series of "eenables." "Eenable us to *so* live." At the third "eenable" there came the blare of a hunting horn down by the river. The hounds came tumbling around the house, and some of the more venturesome leaped on the constable's kneeling figure, frantic for the chase. But the constable continued earnest in prayer. With each "eenable" he would reach back a long leg and kick a hound off the gallery, punctuating his slow sentences — a light kick for a comma, a mighty kick for a period. Lee, kneeling beside me, I could see was uneasy. And when a fortuitous kick was followed by a piercing yelp he turned and cried reproachfully, "Pappy! Ye damned nigh kilt *Tod!*"

The constable closed hastily on an "eenable" and rose from his knees in exasperation. "Dad bum thim boys across ther river! Ther hain't nothin' ter hunt now! I 've a good mint ter go over 'n' arrest 'em. I 'lows they 's drinkin'."

"I reckon, Joe," said Grandpap gently, "ye hain't cleaned up yit, *en*-tire."

The constable changed the subject. "Now you-all

jist wait twell arter dinner ter-morrow, an' I 'll take ye ter Springdale so 's ye need n't git inter harness 'ith the leetle wagon." We knew the futility of trying to make a mountaineer understand that we loved our double harness, and the unfrequented ways, and so agreed to wait.

"Goin' in fur thet horrer ye sint fur in the mail-order Wush Book, Joe? Don't forgit my terbaccer."

"Yeah, I aims ter stay the night 'ith Arreny's brother thar. He 's got er garage, an' he 'll show you-all the new co't house an' ther fire deepartmint."

After breakfast Peter went with the constable to see his Holsteins; but I grudged an hour away from Grandpap, and followed him to the back yard to admire the new washing machine he had presented to Arreny for a "Chris'mus gif'."

"Though aimin' fur the best, I air sometime wushful I 'd agot Arreny sumpen else. I allers hes ter grind hit," he said.

The back yard was clean and grassy, and shaded by gnarled apple trees which appeared to have been pruned with an axe.

"What a pity to mutilate those good old trees like that!" I cried.

"Whut 's the matter 'ith 'em?" asked Grandpap. "I mutulated thim myself. But effen ye knows a better way, arter I quit grindin' I 'll git ther hatchet an' mutulate lak ye say."

Arreny built a fire under a great iron kettle, and filled the machine with the best linen. "What a good housekeeper your daughter is!" I said to Grandpap.

"Yeah, Arreny 's a good womern — a leetle more savin 'n I 'm ust ter. Now Arreny jist won't putt enough soap in ther machine ter wash clo'es quick. Whin her back 's turned I allers slips in er piece I carries in my pocket, en she niver knows hit." He produced half a bar of yellow soap, but at that moment Arreny looked into the machine. To cover his embarrassment Grandpap bit a chew from his plug of tobacco and slipped it with the soap into his pocket. "I niver did think ter see the day I 'd chaw store terbaccer, but," he sighed, "they don't raise hit no more hyarabouts."

Arreny replenished the fire under the kettle, and Grandpap hurriedly slipped something from his pocket into the machine, and cranked rapidly. I sat on a bench and listened to the murmur of the bees in the "yarb gyarden," and watched the vanishing mists above the encircling hills. Arreny came and looked into the machine. "Kingdom come! Whativer 's the matter 'ith thim clo'es! They is as yaller as pumpkins! They is plumb ruint!"

Grandpap peered in anxiously. "I 'low," he said, "thar must a ben some chemikile in thet store soap ye use, Arreny. I reckon hit spiled 'ith ther heat."

"Wal, I cain't bile 'em lak thet. I 'low I 'll hev ter tote 'em ter the river an' wash 'em. Ther well air most give out." And Arreny sighed wearily.

"Let Grandpap and me take them to the river," I

said. "I 've seen foreign women wash in the river. It seemed great fun."

Grandpap and I carried the heavy basket of wet linen — a stick through the handle — to Wanderin' River; and Grandpap shook his head sadly. "I 'm gittin' ole an' childish. I hain't ter be trusted no more a-tall. I reckon I th'owed in ther wrong piece. Now I hain't got no terbaccer, an' my Sunday shirt 's as yaller as gold! I ort ter not putt hit on yis'dy!"

We sat happily on the grassy bank and let the busy little waterfall wash the linen on the clean stones.

"Fish?" said Grandpap, in reply to a question of mine. "No 'm, whin we wants fish ter eat we seines 'em. Oh, ye wants ter ketch 'em! Wal, ye git Joe ter drap you-all out whar the road goes up ter Nixt Widnesday's. Hit air jist three whoops an' a holler round ther mounting. Hit 'll not mis-putt Nixt Widnesday ter hev you-all stop by an' fish in thet-thar lake in Wanderin' River whar he don't 'low nobody ter seine."

"Next Wednesday! Is that his name?"

"No 'm, his name is rightly Robert Cole, but iverbody calls him Nixt Widnesday. Ye see, he air a friendly man, but he air plumb set agin tradin' an' business. But he raises mighty fine stock, an' whin inybody kims ter buy a cow-brute offen him he allers says, 'Kim over nixt Widnesday. I cain't be pestered 'ith no-'count things ter-day.' An' hit air ther truth thet he won't pay nobody fur nothin' only

on a Widnesday. He 'lows he cain't spar' the time
frum fishin' en readin', an' hev his time broke inter
thataway. He air a widder man, an' his onliest
chile 's a gal.

"Nixt ter Dottie Crawford, Burnis wuz ther
purtiest gal in ther settlemint, an' er long ways the
peartest. She teached Chicken Bristle one term.
One day Link Martin he wint over 'n' tole Nixt
Widnesday he war goin' ter marry Burnis. Hit lak
ter kilt Nixt Widnesday. . Ye see, he 'd rared up
Burnis kinder lak a boy an' made kinder a friend
outen her. He jist booted Link outen the house.
Some claims he pursooed him 'ith a shotgun. But
thet, I 'low, is er lie. He air a plumb peaceable man.
But I hed hit frum Link's own mouth thet arter he
booted him outen ther house he set out arter him an'
ketches him at ther ford. Link claims he war a-
cryin', an' he says : 'Link, I hain't no manner o' right
ter stand in Burnis's way. An' effen she 's choosed
sich a damned, dumb hill-billy as you, she got a right
ter her choosin'. But I don't aim ter set round
waitin' an' grievin', countin' the days twell she gone.
Ye kin hev her effen ye 'll take her by nixt Widnesday.' Shore 'nuff, they wuz married at Springdale
nixt Widnesday. I wusht I could read lak Nixt
Widnesday. Though I don't wush ter be witched
by readin' lak him."

·"It might be a pastime for you, Grandpap."

Grandpap, in that intent way of the very old, fixed
his eyes on a green frog proudly swelling on the bank.

"No 'm, I don't 'low as I needs er pastime. Ye see, whin ye is ole lak me, iver leetle thing is cur'ous-lak. The fust long shadder o' the mounting on the grass in ther evenin' is wuth watchin' now, an' er frog er a hop-toad is a cur'ous animile lak me — hyar ter-day, an' gone lak me ter-morrow. No 'm, I wants ter be enabled ter read ter 'spute 'ith Arreny. She reads ther Bible ter me a heap, an' dawggone effen I don't b'lieve she makes up some o' hit ter prove her Apostolic p'ints! — Dinged effen I don' b'lieve thet shirt 's comin' clean!"

We set out at once after dinner for the new "horrer," all three of us sitting in the wide spring seat of the jolt wagon, Sisyphus in the back, weighted with jars of honey and muscadine jelly for ourselves and for Next Wednesday. While John, frantic with delight to be on the road again, chased elusive rabbits through the bordering cotton fields.

"Cotton," said Peter, "seems to be the only crop which really interests you farmers here."

"Yeah, I do 'low thet cotton hes kinder witched iverbody."

"No wonder!" I cried. "From its first pale, lovely blossom, through its squaring, down to its snowy, venerable head, it is fascinating!"

The constable leaned down and spat over the wheel with the wind.

"I hain't aimin' ter 'spute whut yer say, ma 'm, but I 'lows thet cotton hain't no fascinatering plant ter me. Whut 'ith the army worm, an' the boll weevil,

an' ther low price o' cotton, an' no way o' storin' hit,
an' hevin' ter sell it right off, ter pay fertilizer bills,
not ter mintion doctor bills, a man don't scurcely git
back his seed.   An' hit works a turble weight on a
rinter.   Ye see, a rinter hes got ter putt in cotton er
he cain't git no place.   No 'm, I 'm 'bout turned
agin' cotton.   I 'm a-turnin' ter Bermudy grass an'
cow-brutes."

The constable slumped down in the seat, slackened
the lines up the long steep hill, and shifted his quid
of tobacco to his off cheek.   Peter felt for a cigarette,
and I settled the camp pillow at my back.

"Hit war a creepin' cold day last fall, an' I war
a-ridin' right erlong hyar.   I rickolec' hit wuz jist
afore I kim ter Chicken Bristle schoolhouse.   I 'se
a-settin' in this hyar wagon, 'ith the lines atween my
knees, joggin' erlong tryin' ter play er tune on a
French harp I 'd bought fur Lee frum sellin' my
cotton fur 'bout half whut it orter a brung.   The
mules shied, an' thar war Hinry Embry standin' in
ther road.   He 's a rinter frum over on Push Mounting.   Hit war chillin' cold, an' his ole coat war tore
an' flappin' in ther wind, an' Hinry air a widder man,
an' he looked pow'ful puny.   I stopped the mules,
an' Hinry got in.   He 'lowed he 'd walked in ter
Springdale 'cause one o' his mules war crippled.   He
hed ter git medicine fur his leetlest boy.   He claimed
Jimmy war pow'ful sick, an' he 'lowed he wus n't
goin' ter live.   He said he war n't sleepin' none
hisself, an' the neighbors wuz plumb wore out 'ith

settin' up. I tole him hit would n't mis-putt me none ter ride on home 'ith him an' set up. We 'd stop by an' tell Arreny. Thin, lak a dad-bummed fool, ter kinder git his mind offen hit, I says : —

"'You take the lines, Hinry, an' I 'll make a stob at thet tune I hyard on the phoneygraph at Nash's drug store ter-day. I 'm takin' the French harp ter Lee. He 's ben wantin' one so bad he kin taste hit! Nash 'lowed a feller named Susie made the tune up. Quare name. Hit 's titled "King Cotton," an' hit goes sumpen lak this.' An' I says cheerful-lak, 'Hurrah fur King Cotton!' an' I lets out a blow. Hinry he th'owed down the lines, an' stud up in ther wagon, an' shuck his fist at ther sky, an' he snarls lak a trapped varmint : 'Ye-e-ah! Blow yer damn ole harp fur King Cotton! See thet ole tore-down schoolhouse by ther crick! Three months school, an' our chillun a-growin' up ignerant hill-billies lak us afore 'em! Ye knows hit 's so! They 'll allers be too pore an' too ignerant to be nothin' else. They 's a-hoein' an' a-choppin' an' a-pickin' fur King Cotton! Hurrah fur King Cotton! Hurrah fur King Cotton!'

"He kep' a-yellin' hit lak a screech owl twell ther mules tried ter run. And he wint on a-standin' up an' wavin' his arms, an' pintin' at ther cotton fiel's : 'Nary man kin rint er acre o' land lessen he promises ter putt in cotton. Cotton! A-plantin' no cawn, no grain fur ter feed his stock ner his fambly — not even time fur a gyarden. Hurrah fur King Cotton! My womern!' he screeched. 'Dead 'ith her babe!

Drug thim heavy sacks in pickin' season twell her time — fur King Cotton! An' now Jimmy, peartest of 'em all — jist six — his mammy aimed ter make a preacher outen him — a-pickin' cotton 'ith his sore leetle fingers twell he whimper in his sleep lak a dreamin' houn'! Dyin' now. Hurrah fur King Cotton!' An' he sets down suddent an' starts ter cry. Thar 'peared ter be nothin' I could rightly say, so I says hit.

"Arreny she pack up some vittles an' some healin' yarbs, an' we gits ter Hinry's by chore time. But, shucks! Ther minute I seen Jimmy I knowed thar wus n't nothin' ter do but wait fur ther Angel o' Death. He wuz plumb burnt up 'ith the fever, an' he did n't know nobody, an' his leetle hands wuz pickin' cover a'ready. We et a snack, an' the neighbor womern wint home an' tuck the other chillun. Hinry wuz plumb wore out, an' wint ter sleep in ther room on a pallet. Hit war creepin' cold, an' ther wind riz, an' hit blowed th'ough ther cracks an' called as mou'nful as hants down ther chimbly. I wint out an' found some logs an' piled 'em in ther fireplace, an' sittled down ter read some in Hinry's Bible on ther stand table. I knowed thar war no use o' pesterin' Jimmy 'ith medicine. He could n't swaller no more.

"'Bout midnight, all o' a suddent Jimmy sets up an' calls loud: 'Pappy! Pappy! I picked forty pounds ter-day!' An' he died 'ith ther perroudist smile on his face I iver seen on ther face o' ther dead.

"Hinry he wakes up, an' he grabbed me an' shuck me lak a rat! He yelled: 'Jimmy wanted *me*! I heerd him! He called fur me! An' I war n't thar! An' he 's gone foriver! Dern ye! Why n't ye wake me!' Thin all of a suddent he says, pow'ful pitiful: 'Whut 'd he say, Joe? Whut 'd Jimmy say ter me?'

"I choked up, but I tells him: 'Hinry, ye heerd him. He says, "Pappy! Pappy! I hyar ther angels a-callin' me!"'

"Yeas, sir, I lied jist lak thet! 'Ith my hand on Hinry's Bible, an' right in ther room 'ith ther dead! But I 'low as I done hit fur Hinry — er fur thet air King Cotton — niver could deetermine rightly whicht. But I niver tole Arreny! Hit 'd most kill Arreny ter know I lied in thim sarcumstances. No 'm, I 'low I 'm plumb th'ough 'ith cotton, lessen sumpen changes.

"Hyar 's you-all's road up ter Nixt Widnesday's. Shore you-all don't wanter go on ter Springdale? To my mind he air got ther lonesomest place in ther mountings, an' it 'pears lak jist three whoops an' er holler up thar, but you-all 'll scurcely make hit by sundown. All right, thin. I reckon we-all won't meet no more in this worl'. Far' ye well, an' the Lord's blessin' on ye both!"

We gave one last shuddering look at the green fields of cotton, and pushed Sisyphus along the white sand between thickets of laurel, under the arching trees.

.

But after a while the feel of the good earth under our feet, the whisper of the leaves above us, the laughter of the little stream where John lapped gratefully, all stole upon us again. The old merciless, generous, capricious, changeless mother of us all knows best how to lull her own children to forgetfulness. And we pushed on, comforted, up the steep way to Next Wednesday.

XI

NEXT WEDNESDAY

It was a long way to Next Wednesday's, and the shadows fell cold as we pushed the reluctant Sisyphus up the steep trail. We rested a moment, tempted to make camp, and looked down into the dim valley below where already evening "cookin' fires" were lighted.

There should be another name by which to designate smoke in the mountains. For it is not smoke as city dwellers know it — dull stifling clouds, breath of giants enslaved. No — straight and gallant mountain smoke rises in the valley, exquisitely, unbelievably blue, an azure incense from the hearth of home, seeking ineffectually the paler sky where the first star burns. All day the August forest fires are pearly gray in the distance, flaming in sudden glory at nightfall. For in that soft haze the hardwood trees smoulder to ashes, but when the night wind rises, the proud pines are caught, and die at once in fierce crackling flames, leaving erect their defiant charred skeletons.

And always the scent, the gipsy lure, of brush burning. Witchery so potent that ever after its very memory must be guarded, lest through some city window with the roar of the world there steal a perfume calling imperiously to a man entrapped, and he should follow with quick cowardice — a soul possessed.

John, who had preceded us around the turn of the road, came running back announcing that adventure was ahead. So we took heart and pushed on rapidly. And there, a little way down the mountain, we saw a log house above the black line of Wanderin' River, and a man sweeping the bare space before his door with a "bresh broom." For no mountaineer likes the grass too near his dwelling. Presently the man sat on his door stone and lighted his pipe. We never before had seen a mountain man smoking, though sometimes we had found an old woman crouched in the chimney corner smoking a corn-cob pipe, or a youth defiantly puffing a cigarette.

Next Wednesday must have seen us descending the lane, but he made no sign, and I wondered if he were a recluse who might resent our coming. As we drew near Peter called : —

"Hello! Is this Next Wed —" Then to me, desperately, "What 's his name? What 's his name besides Next Wednesday?"

"Cole," I answered.

"Is this Mr. Cole's place?"

The man arose at once and cried: "Kim right on in. I wuz sorter lookin' fur you-all ter-night. Word kim thet ye wuz at Joe Ross's, an' ye wuz jist a-roamin'. I 'lowed thet Grandpap 'd head you-all fur hyar. I 've et, but I lef' ye sumpen in the kitchen. You-all jist enter."

We followed him gratefully through the dogtrot into the kitchen, where he lighted a wall lamp.

Next Wednesday was neither so tall nor so gaunt as the average mountain man, and his quiet, smooth-shaven face was lined with laughter wrinkles. Above the fine straight nose of the mountaineer were amused gray eyes turned down at the corners. His hair waved in an iron-gray mane, and his mouth was firm but mobile. A mountain man is accustomed to use his lips so little in speech that they seem as useless for speaking as our ears are now for wagging.

There were cold vegetables, ham, and fruit on the table, with "flour bread" and sassafras tea hot and spicy on the stove. Peter went out and brought in the jars of honey and of muscadine jelly that Grandpap had sent to Next Wednesday.

"Thet 's plumb neighborly o' Grandpap. Him an' Joe is good neighbors. A leetle lakin' in ambitiern — jist contint 'ith their own environmint, ner keerin' fur the worl' outside. They scoots the idee o' readin' inything but ther Bible. You-all kin read, I reckon?"

"Yes, we can," said Peter.

During our stay with Next Wednesday we were always delighted to watch him search about in his mind for the exact word, and then call it anything his fancy dictated. For many of the words Next Wednesday meets in his reading he has never heard pronounced, nor ever will.

At last Peter said, "If you will show me some convenient spot to set our tent I 'll make camp before the moon is down."

"Seein' as you-all is kinder gipsies, I thort ye might lak ter sleep in my tree house. I swep' hit out ter-day. Hit 's in a mounstrous oak jist over the river. But you-all is plumb welcome ter sleep in ther house effen ye 'd ruther."

"Oh, how lovely!" I cried. "The tree house will be delightful!"

Next Wednesday gave me a smile of approval.

"I seen a picter o' a tree house in a paper, an' I 'lows I improved on hit. Fur I hung hit on wire so hit swings 'ith ther tree in ther wind — a mite more lak natur'. I lays out thar some nights ter look at ther stairs in ther cawnsilliations, an' pawnders how fur off they is, an' how het up we air, runnin' round lak crazy ants. Effen you-all hain't too wore out, kim inter the room an' see my books. I takes two papers, but they hain't lak books."

We went across the dogtrot in the dark and waited while he lighted with great care a large lamp with bright red roses on its shade. The room was unexpectedly prim. The log walls were whitewashed, and before the cavernous rock fireplace was a rug of dyed goatskins. The inevitable snowy bed was absent, but there was a rustic easy-chair by the table with the lamp, and I noted with surprise the white starched curtains at the windows. On the wall under a silent clock was a shelf holding a dozen books. We examined them curiously, somehow reverently.

"I heired thim books frum Mr. Leonard. Hit war nigh onter fifty yar ergo whin he fust kim an' teached ther school an' dwelt 'ith us. He war frum the North an' hed lung trouble whin he kim ter the mountings. He died in this hyar room. 'Peared lak nobody keered fur thim books o' hisn but me. An' nobody writ him er line the endurin' time he war hyar. He war young, an' sence I growed up I hev marveled at hit. I 'low I 'd not keered fur the books effen he hed n't read 'em aloud all ther time, an' tole me so murch about 'em."

"They are great books," said Peter; "the best in the world."

Next Wednesday's eyes shone.

"I don't bring nobody inter this room lessen they kin read. Hit air jist a notion."

Never, I thought, since the exiled youth closed his eyes forever in this room, has a stranger given a glance of approval or of recognition to the little shelf of books below the dumb old clock.

Next Wednesday went on proudly: "Hyar 's thim plays o' William Shakespeare. Mr. Leonard

he read 'em out loud an' explained 'em twell I most
got 'em by heart.   They jist fills up ther house 'ith
folks on winter nights in hyar.   Hit air miny a long
yar sence I heerd a voice readin' 'em out loud.
Burnis, ner Viney, my womern, did n't seem lak they
keered fur 'em.   Did you-all iver hyar o' a American
man named Mr. Emerson?"

"Yes, we have," answered Peter.

"Mr. Leonard wuz jist plumb wropped up in thet
man.   But I 'lows I lak Hinry D. Thoreau best.
Mr. Emerson seems kinder furder off an' chillier.
Hyar 's Epictetus.   I read him a heap arter Viney
died an' Burnis married.   An' — but you-all kin
kim in an' read 'em whilst ye air hyar.   An' effen
we ketch ther moon we best go.   Ther tree house air
jist er step down ther hill."

Though sometimes when either of us would pur-
posely falter in a quotation Next Wednesday would
finish it, he never once spoke of anything he read.
His life in the temple of the books was shut away
from his everyday existence.   He had been alone in
his devotions too long and had renounced the hope
of ever sharing his sacred joy with another.   And
now the gates of his soul were too rusted to open.
And after his one remark about Mr. Emerson we
had hoped for the illumination of a fresh mind.   But
only once did he ever allude to the books again, and
to this day it saddens me that we were not able to
find the key to this secret chamber of his mind.

A mighty oak stretched great black arms over the

river to the sky. We climbed high into the tree where a small railed platform rested securely, fastened with wires. Unwelcome intruders in this city of beetles and birds and little hiding wild creatures, we spent a deservedly white night. But by far too good a night for unconsciousness. And a night in a swaying tree over the river and under the stars brings rest without surrender to sleep. Throughout the sweet silence of the night some waterfowl — some mateless bird — called incessantly, "Come back! Come back!" till the cry was hoarse with pain.

"And those eternal whippoorwills!" said Peter. "Will they never cease complaining of the long hours of labor and the high cost of raw material?"

"The human note in the night's symphony," I sighed. "Perhaps there are not enough insects to go round. And whippoorwills are homeless birds."

Toward morning, when the pulse of life beats low, there was silence and we slept; to awaken refreshed and to look down on John industriously picking burrs from his tail. For once he had deserted Sisyphus and had gone for a wild night on the river; and he confessed as much with ashamed appealing eyes.

How good life is! And how gallantly our breakfast fire crackles and flames! Set not too near the dew-drenched morning-glories or the sad purple blossoms of the cross vine.

Next Wednesday appeared presently with a jug.

"Hyar's a leetle lift over frum afore Joe Ross turned constable. Hit air good liquor." And it was.

"Hit air er fine mornin' fur fishin', effen you-all aims ter fish.   Won't thet John spile the fishin'?"

"Well," I admitted, "he does get rather excited when I catch a very large fish.   But Peter does not care to fish.   He'll watch us and take my fish off the hook and keep John."

Next Wednesday grinned amusedly.   "A heap o' fun laid out fur Peter this mornin', I 'low."

I admitted this too.

A little way to the south the river widened into a small natural lake.   The banks were sloping, grassy, and strewn with boulders.   Peter lay on the bank near us with John on his chain and a book beside him.   Next Wednesday spat with commendable precaution on the brown hackle I gave him from my book of flies.   I meant to try for an August trout. And after several strikes and some small fish I landed two beauties and reeled in my line.

"I laks ther way ye fishes, Sister," said Next Wednesday; "puttin' the leetle ones back, an' quittin' whin ye gits ernough.   I mean ter git some o' thim barbless hooks.   But I don't seem ter hev no luck 'ith this hyar fly.   Hit air drowned out.   I 'low I'll jist set my pole by ther bank fur er cat. Some folks don't lak cat.   But I kin fry er cat twell inybody 'll lak it."

Across the ford below us splashed a brown mule that stopped to drink.   A woman rode man-fashion and without a saddle.   She carried a heavy basket on her arm.

"Thet 's Burnis," said Next Wednesday.   "She 's
the beatinist gal!   She 's hyard you-all is hyar an'
she 's rid over 'ith some fraish braid an' vittles, not
a-waitin' fur Widnesday.   I 'low hit 's got spread
eround 'bout thet fiddle you-all carries.   Burnis air
a natcherel musicianer.   She kin make this hyar
jazz music outern iny tune she iver hyars oncet.
Whin she married I kep' the orgin I 'd bought her.
I keeps hit in ther room fur thim as don't read.   I 'll
git her ter light an' tie an' go up an' play some fur
you-all."

Burnis (I found her name in a book, and it was
Berenice) was young and lithe, and her mouse-
colored hair hung in ringlets about a pale face of
recondite beauty.   She had her father's blue-gray
eyes drawn down at the corners, but in place of his
amused, almost quizzical expression there was a
look in the girl's face as if she weighed her every
word — and yours.   She did not dismount.

"No, Pappy," she said in a surprisingly low voice,
as deep as a cello, "I cannot stay.   Link is in ther
hay.   But I hyard — heard thar wuz comp'ny an'
I brung — I brought some fraish braid an' some
huckleberry pies.   Howdy.   I 'low I 'd lak ter see
you-all's leetle wagon.   It must be interesting."
After a moment's conversation with her father she
said : —

"I reckon I 'll go on.   But Link an' me — I
mebby 'll kim over after chorin'."   Then to me in
the impressive tone always used in this formal adieu

in the mountains, "Kim on an' go home 'ith me."
I replied correctly, "*You* come."

We committed many gaucheries before we came
to understand that this invitation only signifies that
one is accepted, and should never be taken literally.
One is neither expected to accept nor to regret, but
to reply heartily, "*You* come."

As the graceful figure disappeared across the ford,
Next Wednesday chuckled: "Hit allers tickles me
ter hyar Burnis try ter talk corrict. She knows how,
but she hain't got no practice. Now me — effen I
kin find er nacherel word I uses it. Course effen
thar hain't none I uses a corrict one. But thim
grammar words ain't p'inted somehow lessen they
is erlong 'ith ithers lak 'em in er book. Fur instant
— whin I says, 'I 'm jist plumb wore out,' hit air
more meanful thin, 'I am very fati-*gued*.' Hit ain't
p'inted."

"It ain't, Next Wednesday. I mean Mr. Cole."

"You-all need n't primp up yer mouths ter say
nothin' but Nixt Widnesday. Ye 'll niver hyar me
called nothin' else. Ye see, I jist saves iverthin'
thet 's plumb pesterin' fur one day in ther week an'
gits th'ough 'ith hit. Jist happened ter light on
Widnesday as ther onlucky day. Now humans is
awful interestin' ter me, but not whin they is tradin'
hosses, ner payin' debts, ner buyin' cow-brutes.
Dinged effen I 'll let my life be et inter lak thet! I
pays fur hit by bein' called quare. My thoughts,
ye might say, is medierms of exchange — an' seems

lak they don't *com*-pile no intrust. I 'low, though,
hit kinder shames Burnis. Burnis air a mite quare
herself. Ye see, she war my onliest chile, an' her
mammy died whin she war six, an' I riz her up lak
a gal an' lak a boy too. We hes a releegious feelin'
'bout womern in ther mountings, an' we expects 'em
ter jestify hit. An' thet 's too hard on iny human.
So I tries ter train up Burnis ter do whut she dinged
please so 's folks 'd git used ter hit. But she jist
growed up plumb proper an' jist lak iverbody else.
I 'lows I war a mite disapp'inted. But she air lak
her mammy afore her — jist nacherelly good-
behaved. Though I did larn Burnis ter make up
her own mind 'bout inything, an' Link ner me hain't
got nothin' ter say whin she does. Course we both
presints argymints. But I got more sinse 'n ter
break in on martial relations. They is best let
erlone, er kim at sideways. But we hed a shore-'nuff
battle o' minds over a quistion last summer — I
believe I got er bite! Thim cats take ther bait
slow."

Peter, who found us more interesting since we
were not really fishing, came over and lay on the
sloping green bank.

"Mind telling who won in that battle?" he asked.

"No, I don't mind, though maybe hit ain't a
plumb purty story. But I 'low Sister hyar air lak
Burnis, an' a human effen so *in*-clined. As I wuz
sayin', our womern hain't expected ter step aside in
no partickler frum ther way iver womern hes walked

sence these hyar mountings war settled. Now you take Mattie Porter, fur instant. Mattie Porter lived over in Shady Cove jist behint Wildcat. Ther hain't, you might say, no road inter ther Cove, an' dinged effen I don't 'low as they 'd scorn a womern even now thet 'd wear short hair thar.

"Shucks! Thet pairch got erway 'ith ther last o' my rabbit bait! Gotter putt on er worm now. Wal, Mattie war a ole maid not ter say purty, but a nice old maid 'bout twinty-eight yar ole. She waited on her ole gran'mammy whut wuz baidridden, an' her brother runs ther place. Hit turned out thet Mattie wuz allers a-rebellin' inside; an' one day she tuck the idee thet she wuz wishful ter see furder out o' ther Cove — out ter whar ther sun goes down. So she goes over ter ther highest place an' clomb inter ther big tree they calls ther Big Oak. She kim up frum tother side an' did n't figger on hit 's bein' a Satidy an' min a-settin' roun' in front o' the post office. One o' thim seen her an' lak a dinged fool he yells, 'Miss Mattie Porter is a-hangin' herself in ther Big Oak!' An' Willie Godbehere he starts a-runnin' an' hollers, 'Cut her down! Cut her down!' An' they runs up ther hill a-brandishern a knife, an' Mattie 's so outdone she falls outern ther tree an' sprains her ankle afore she explains thet she jist wanted ter see furder."

"Poor Miss Mattie!" I cried. "Does she live in Shady Cove now?"

"No. Her granny dies an' leaves her a leetle

piece o' land an' she sells hit ter her brother an'
lights right out ter her ant in Texas. Course she
war a talked-about womern frum thet day in ther
tree. But Mattie Porter war one ole maid as hed
ther ineetitive ter git outen her environmint, an' I
allers hel' up fur her, an' so did Burnis."

"But about that battle of wits last summer," said
Peter.

"Yeah, hit war a important battle, though takin'
place outer sight in Link an' me. Folks hes different
idees o' ther importance o' things. Hit war over
Dottie Crawford. Preacher Crawford he lives over
this side o' the crossroads store, an' Dottie war ther
onliest chile at home. The rest jist got up an' lit
out. Dottie, — her name war Dorcas, but iverbody
but her mammy an' pappy called her Dottie, — she
war a leetle thing 'ith eyes a-lookin' sideways, an'
dimples, an' allers a-prancin' on her toes. Now
Burnis war thought purty, an' iver feller war
a-sparkin' her 'ith the idee o' whut a likely womern
she 'd make fur a wife. But Dottie wuz one o' thim
yaller-haided, rovin'-eyed gals as makes iver man
thet gits a sight o' her glad he 's young er mournful
thet he hain't. Shucks! Burnis wuz jist lak a loaf
o' flour braid beside a pint o' moonshine! — Thar
goes my pole!" he cried, recovering it in time.
"Hain't thet ther biggest, cleanest cat ye iver see?
Ye wait twell hit 's mealed an' fried, an' taste hit
erlong o' yer trout! Now effen I ain't gone an' lef'
my smokin' terbaccer at ther house!"

"Try this," said Peter, hastily crumbling a cigarette. "I take it that even gentlemen of the mountains prefer blondes?"

"Yeah?" said Next Wednesday vaguely, lighting his pipe and leaning back against a rock. "Though ther onliest one thet war pledged ter Dottie war Mark Spotswood — an' him Dottie war a-foolin'. Wal, ole Preacher Crawford, he would n't let Dottie go nowhar lessen she war a-settin' atween thim two in ther jolt wagon. An' purty soon thar war rumors. Some 'lowed thet Dottie war a-crawlin' outer the winder at night, an' goin' off in cars ter low-down dances at Wildcat — some said plumb ter Springdale. Hit finally got ter Preacher Crawford's yurs an' hell wuz a-poppin'! Somehow jist fur the reason they war plumb onlike, Burnis an' Dottie thought a heap o' one another. But 'bout thet time Burnis marries Link Martin — whut fur I niver could rightly deetermine, lessen by niver sayin' nothin' he lets on he's thinkin'. Inyways, they hel' Dottie in lak thet fur bout er yur an' thin suddint we hyars thet Dottie hed runned erway 'ith somebody ter Nashville. Niver nobody knowed rightly who tuck her — she niver tolt even Burnis. Somehow I allers hed a pow'ful soft spot in my heart fur Dottie." Here Peter grinned impolitely. Next Wednesday gave him a keen glance from his drawn-down eyes and took a puff at his pipe.

"Yeah," he went on slowly. "Thar's sumpen 'bout a gal lak Dottie Crawford thet gits er man. I 'low

Eve pranced round on leetle toes an' looked sideways. Course some o' us, Peter, a-backin' up our prides, 'lows a gal lak thet is hidin' a turble fine soul; an' they 'lows as they is ther onliest one thet hes diskivered hit. As I says, Peter, they is some lak thet."

I suppressed a giggle, and Peter threw a pine cone at me. But he made the *amende honorable*, and said, "You are a mighty honest man as well as a wise one, Next Wednesday."

"I 'lows we's all purty murch alike." And, gracefully acknowledging the apology, he said, "Kin ye crum'le another o' thim cigarettes, Peter?"

Next Wednesday struck a match carefully on a little rock, slowly puffed at his pipe, and went on: "'Bout this time Buddy Wear he wint ter Nashville 'ith his hawgs, an' whin he kim back he claimed thet he seen Dottie a-dancin' at one o' thim kafes whar the feller he sold 'em to tuck him. He 'lowed as Dottie war the purtiest leetle thing he iver seen, an' war plumb onree-pintent, an' kim over 'n speaks ter him right frindly-lak, an' 'peared downright happy in sin. Howsomiver, he 'lowed that the Bible says 'the wages o' sin is death.' I axed him effen he reeminded Dottie o' thet; an' he 'lowed he disremembered hit at ther time but hit kim ter him strong ther nixt mornin' whin he tuck the train fur home, an' he wuz pestered that he hed n't thought o' hit before."

Peter laughed, and the old man's eyes drew down at the corners and twinkled.

"As I war a-sayin', hit war August, jest 'bout this time — an' sudden hit war rumored that Dottie Crawford hed kim back home a-dyin'. A furrin ole womern hed brung Dottie on the cars ter Springdale an' wint right on th'ough hersilf. Ole Doc Johnson thet brung Dottie inter ther worl', he drives out 'ith her to Preacher Crawford's an' makes 'em take Dottie in. 'Lowed he 'd hev the law on 'em effen they did n't — en could, too. Though thar I misdoubts he lied. Inyway they putt Dottie in ther front room an' shet all ther shutters lak as they war a-hidin' a mounstrosity stid er a leetle dyin' bird. Doc he driv out iver day an' he tolt me her mammy ner her pappy niver spoke er word ter her — jist give her the medicine he lift an' done whut he tolt 'em ter do.

"Now ye knows effen Dottie 'd kim back ter the mountings 'ith a chance-chile, some 'd a scorned her, but hit 'd not lasted. Fur a chile is er chile. But ole Granny Jinkins as takes keer o' ther womern whin a chile kims, she wint right over ter Crawford's an' wint home an' 'lowed thet Dottie hed gone agin natur' an' war a murderer. The pore onguided chile hed tuck bad advice.

"Wal, I lay up in ther tree house an' thort o' thet leetle foolish dancin' thing thet hed tried her wings ter git inter ther sun, twell I could n't stand hit no longer. Ye see, Dottie did n't rightly hev no chancet. None o' our young folks hes no chancet iny more. The ole kinds er injoymint is gone. No

more log raisin's whar they kim frum iverwhar an'
hes a frolic fur days at er time. Even ther churches
hain't givin' no more dinner on ther grounds. An'
dances is jist fur low-down folks now — not lak ther
oncet wuz. Iver boy he hes ter save up fur er automobile, an' whin he gits one thar hain't no place ter
go. 'Pears lak folks air suspiciers o' one another
nowadays — they don' lak one another lak they
uster. Town folks scorns our young folks effen they
goes inywhar but ter thim picter shows. An' a
picnic is jist whar folks kin set up places ter sell
things, er gamble at shootin' dolls er somethin' equal
foolish. Dinged effen ther last picnic at Hangin'
Rock wuz n't more lak a fun'ral. Yeah, truth is we
ain't nowhar now. Ole times is plumb gone, an'
onderstan' I hain't a-runnin' down new times; but
mebby us mounting folks hain't ready fur 'em. Kin
ye crum'le another, Peter?"

Peter hastily opened the last of his precious pack-
ages of tailor-mades. Next Wednesday lighted his
pipe and puffed a moment in silence.

"As I war a-sayin', I could n't stand hit no longer,
an' the nixt Widnesday I rid over ter Burnis's an'
led tother mule erlong. I got thar jist at dinner, an'
arter we hed et I says, plumb offhand-lak, 'Burnis, I
'lows as Dottie Crawford 's a frind o' yourn.'

"'Yes,' says Burnis.

"'Wal,' I says, 'a frind 's er frind; an' Dottie air
a-layin' dyin' erlone, fur as I kin larn. Hit ain't
nobody else but Dottie.'

"Hit war the fust gun, ye might say, o' thet battle I tolt ye 'bout. Fur Link he ups an' says : 'I don't 'low as hit 's ther same frind a-tall. Dottie Crawford air a weekid womern an' no lessen er murderer.'

"'Yeah,' I says, 'so wuz David in ther Bible, but God stuck ter him.'

"'Thet war a long time ergo an' we did n't know so murch thim days. Besides, Burnis ain't no God. She air a womern an' my womern! An' ye hain't goin' ter aidge round ter git Burnis ter go over ter Crawford's.'

"'No use gittin' het up, Link,' I says mighty quiet, fur I knowed hit war onwise ter horn in on martial relations. 'But,' I says, kinder thortful-lak, 'somehow I 'lowed thet ye wuz Burnis's man erlong er her bein' yer womern.'

"'I sees yer p'int,' says Link, ca'min' down, 'but Burnis ain't a-goin' ter bring down talk on herself, ner smurch herself a-consartin' 'ith sinners.'

"'I 'm plumb pleased, Link,' I says, 'thet ye gits my p'int; fur Burnis hain't my gal ner yore womern *en*-tire. All I gotter say hit 's er pore frind thet don't stick th'ough trouble an' sin whin needed. An' I brung erlong ole Beck saddled, 'ith some jelly an' blackberry wine in er poke, an' hit 'll not mis-putt me none ter ride over ter Crawford's 'ith Burnis effen she should deecide she hain't no better 'n God.'

"Link he turned white as ther daid an' he clinches down on ther jelly glass he war drinkin' outer twell hit busted an' cut his hand.

"Burnis hed n't let out er word. She gits up an' ties up Link's hand, an' she clars ther table an' washes ther dishes an' wipes out ther dishpan an' wrings out ther rag an' hangs hit careful outside the door. Thin she goes in tother room an' kims out in a clean dress an' ties on her white sunbunnit. Link did n't say a word; neither did Burnis; neither did I. But jist as we war ridin' off Burnis calls, 'Link, effen I hain't home airly will you give the ole settin' hin some cool water?

"'All right,' says Link. He knowed he war whooped.

"We rid up ter ther house, an' lighted an' tied. I waited ter see whut 'd happen 'fore I wint back. Miss Crawford kim round frum whar she war pickin' beans. Burnis says, 'I kim ter see Dottie.' Miss Crawford says, 'Dorcas is in ther room,' an' walks right back ter ther bean patch. An' I knowed thet Preacher Crawford he war assistin' at er *ree*-vival over at Laurel-hell Holler. So Burnis wint in an' I rid back a leetle lighter in my mind. 'Bout sundown Burnis hed n't kim back, so I rid over arter her. Dottie war daid an' laid out."

Next Wednesday was silent. He knocked the ashes from his pipe and looked down on Wanderin' River. Then —

"Kin ye crum'le another, Peter?"

He lighted his pipe and smoked awhile in silence.

"As I was sayin', all ther way home Burnis jist rid erlong on ole Beck 'ith her bunnit over her face,

though hit war jist atween daylight an' dark an'
thet mule o' mine kicked up an' like ter slid frum
under me pretindin' ter skeer. At my house she
says, 'Pappy, I 'll go in 'ith you; Link 'll kim fur
me arter chorin'.'

"I tuck her in ther kitchen an' sets her in ther
leetle chur whar she ust ter set whin troubled, an'
I th'owed in er pine knot fur a flash an' made her a
cup o' store tea. She drinks hit an' suddent begins
ter laugh an' thin ter cry. I knowed thet she hed
hystrikes, an' wint out an' gits er feather an' burns
hit on the stove, an' she laughs an' says, 'Pappy!
Hit war tur'ble! Tur'ble! Hit 'll hant me foriver!
I did n't call on Dottie ter reepint ner nothin'! An'
Dottie died whilst I war —' An' she begins ter cry
agin.

"'Burnis,' I says, 'I riz ye up 'ith sinse! Ye jist
begin quiet-lak an' tell hit all, an' thin we 'll jedge.'

"An' Burnis says: 'The room wuz all dark an'
hot an' foul-smellin', an' pore Dottie wuz thrashin'
round all fevered up an' her eyes a-starin'. "I
knowed ye 'd kim, Burnis!" she says. An' I drops
down by the baid an' I says, "I 'm hyar, Dottie.
Kin I do sumpen fur ye?" An' Dottie says, "Open
up thim shutters an' let ther light in, fur Gawd's
sake!" I did, an' bathed her face an' hit seemed
ter soothe her. An' she says, "Take that sorry
picter offen ther table by ther baid an' th'ow hit
behint ther orgin!" Hit war a framed picter in
leetle pine cones o' the Lord whoopin' folks outern

the temple 'ith a leetle whoop. I tuck hit erway an' Dottie says, "Go over ter my suitcase in ther corner an' open hit. Hyar 's the key on a string on my neck. Now ye git out thet picter on top an' putt hit hyar on ther stand table." Pappy, I jest felt lak I could n't tech hit! Though hit war a picter o' a biggoty man in a fine frame. Dottie she laughs an' she says : "Ye need n't be so skeered ter tech hit! He air not a bad man an' he air got er bobcat fur a womern. I 'low ye thinks I air weekid, Burnis. But, Burnis!" she says 'ith her eyes big an' starin' straight afore her, "all the lights a-shinin' an' iverbody standin' easy er movin' fast, not lak hyar jist a-boagin' erlong. An' talkin' soft-lak. I larnt ter talk lak thet right off. An' Burnis! Yer feet jist a-flyin' ter ther music! An' iverbody thinkin' how purty ye is! An' nobody thinkin' ye is bad an' weekid! Go on now an' play some music on the orgin. I 'm jist honin' ter hyar ther sound o' somethin'! Gawd! Hit 's still hyar! Jist er ole rooster thet kims under ther winder an' crows mournful-lak an' thin chuckles low arterward, 'Pore fool! Pore fool!' Whin I goes back —"

"'An' I begins ter cry, fur I knowed Dottie wuz n't a-goin' nowhar iver agin but to her grave. An' I says, "Dottie, ye 'll niver go back!" An' Dottie says : "Sometimes I 'low as I 'd lak ter stay hyar safe in ther mountings — an' effen I war ter let on as I 'd reepinted, an' jist pine erway hyar 'ith iverbody a-scornin' me, mebby they 'd let me stay. But,

Burnis, I could n't stand hit an' I knows hit! Yeah,
I 'lows I 'll go back.   I ort niver to hev kim home.
But I war pow'ful sick, an' thim hosspittles skeers
me — an' — an' — I wanted my mammy!" An'
she lays back in the pillars as white as they wuz, but
she niver shed a tear.   An' her a-wantin' her mammy
an' not gitten a kind word!   "Stop snivelin' an' go
play," she says.

"'I could n't hardly pump the orgin, an' I wuz
cryin' so whin I pulled out ther stops I could n't see
'em.   But I played "Rock of Ages"; an' Dottie
calls out, "Fur Gawd's sake, Burnis, jazz hit!   I
cain't stand no mournful tune lak thet!"   I could n't
see the keys, but I jazzed hit. . Hit war weekid,
Pappy, but I jazzed hit!   An' Dottie kep' a-callin',
"Faster! Faster! Jazz hit, Burnis!"   An' thinkin'
Dottie 'd not notice hit, I changed ter "The Land o'
ther Cloudless Sky," which sounds most lak jazz,
thinkin' Dottie 'd not know the difference, an' hit 'd
not sound so blas*phe*-mous.   But she did, an' laughed
low-lak, an' kep a-sayin', "Jazz hit! Jazz hit,
Burnis!" twell hit war a whisper.

"'Purty soon I hyard Doc Johnson's car at the
gate, an' I turned roun', an', Pappy! Dottie war
a-layin' thar daid! I runs out an' Doc Johnson
kims in an' 'lows the pizen jist reached her heart.
Miss Crawford kims in frum the bean patch, seein'
the Doc's car, an' she looks down at Dottie layin' so
still an' innercent thar, an' she takes off her bunnit
slow-lak an' raises her arms an' lets out one long

screech, an' niver sheds er tear, an' goes slow an'
ca'm an' closes Dottie's eyes. An', Pappy, I let
Dottie die thet erway, jist a-listenin' ter blas*phe*-
mous music! I reckon hit 'll hant me an' darken
my life, Pappy.'

"Right thar I war mighty choosy o' my words.
Fur I reelized thet a idee might abscess a person jist
lak Burnis said an' darken they whole life. So I
says, 'Ye wuz a-prayin' fur Dottie silent, wuz n't ye,
Burnis?' An' she 'lowed she wuz. An' I says:
'Wal, do ye think iny spoken word o' yourn could a
reached Dottie lak askin' God ter speak ter her?
Ther Bible says ter minister ter ther sick, but hit
don' mean maybe ter preach ter 'em only. Ye
made Dottie's pore lonely deathbaid happier 'n
inybody on this yearth could er done. Git down
on yer binded knees an' thank Gawddlemighty ye
war thar in time.'

"Wal, Link kim over an' he war pow'ful gintle, an'
Burnis niver worried no more, only grieved fur
Dottie.

"Preacher Crawford, he would n't let Dottie be
buried in ther churchyard whar all his kin hes laid
since these hyar mountings war fust sittled. But
Joe Ross an' me we made er nice coffin an' Burnis
sint ter Springdale an' got some things ter make hit
purty, an' Dottie looked so kinder satisfied, 'ith a
sorter secret smile lak she knowed hit an' war pleased.
But they buried her on ther hill over by ther road to
ther crossroad store, an' they hain't niver ben no

path ter ther grave sence. They did n't want
nobody at ther buryin', but Burnis an' me an' Link
wint, an' a few pushed in outen cur'osity. Thar
war n't no singin', an' Preacher Crawford he, ye
might say, preached his own gal plumb inter hell!
Hit wuz a hot August mornin', but I hed ther shivers
whilst I listened lak whin I sees a dead rattlesnake
wriggle at sundown arter hit air left fur daid, er whin
a dawg howls at night fur a token. 'Bout in ther
middle o' his reemarks hyar kim Mark Spotswood
— him thet thort he war pledged ter Dottie. He
air a ganglin' lad an' tall, an' he kim lopin' up ther
hill th'ough the pines lak a wild animile. He listens
to Dottie's pappy 'ith his haid th'owed back lak a
wild buck an' whin we all knelt fur prayer I looked
fur Mark ter pick up er rock an' th'ow hit at the
preacher. An' I wint over an' knelt beside him, not
wantin' ther settlemint disgraced.

"Wal, arter thet Preacher Crawford tuck ter goin'
over ther kintry preachin' erbout Abraham a-sacri-
ficin' Isaac. Somehow I hain't meanin' ter be
blas*phe*-mous, but I 'low ther printers got thet story
mixed up. As hit stands hit don't th'ow no good
light on Abraham.

"Mark Spotswood, who wuz aimin' ter be a
preacher, he plumb lost his reeligion thet day at
Dottie's buryin', an' he jist left his mammy who war
a widder womern an' his leetle brother Jody ter make
a crop erlone. I hev hyard they putt in er crop on
cawn braid an' sorghum — they is pore folks. Mark,

he air runnin' wild yit 'ith a low-down crowd at
Laurel-hell Holler, though I seed him oncet in ther
snow a-layin by Dottie's grave. But he air young
yit — jist twinty. Dottie wuz goin' on eighteen
whin she died. Kin ye crum'le another, Peter?"

XII

DREAMS BY WANDERIN' RIVER

"PETER," said Next Wednesday, "kin ye lind me a hand ter git my wagon baid on ther gyears? I 'm wishful ter ride ter ther crossroads ter git ther mail, an' a turn o' corn at ther mill. I 'lowed you-all might lak ter go 'long. Hit air er purty good store."

"There is a motor car — a big one — coming up the road from the south," I said.

"Yeah, hit air young Hall 'ith his new car. Lak 'nuff he 's got ole Doc Johnson an' Jedge Burton in ther back seat. They drives out frequint frum ther goluf grounds this side o' Springdale. — Hold on, Peter, I gotter putt in some bolts first. — Some folks don't lak thim fellers thet knocks round a leetle ball in short pants on ther aidge o' town, fur exercise.

Exercise! Whin we-all is cuttin' sprouts — er ort
ter be. — Look th'ough this box an' see effen thar 's
inither bolt this size, Peter. — But I kinder likes 'em.
I claims ther human. Now ye take Hall, fur instant
— he 's frum ther North an' hes lung trouble. But
ther quare thing 'bout thim rich eddicated folks is
thet they niver talks erbout inything they 's spint
their lives a-findin' out. Sometimes I gits my hopes
riz up er minute, but they gits off on ther farm prob-
lim o' which they knows nothin' — ner, hit 'pears,
nobody else does. Finally hit allers whittles down
to whut 's ther best automobile, er why they hain't
playin' goluf right this partickler day. Effen thet is
all eddicatin kin do fur a man hit air plumb dissi-
p'intin'. I hain't denyin' they knows sumpen else;
but er man ain't got no human right ter shet up lak
a snappin' turkle 'bout whut he knows. — All right,
Peter, let 's git her on."

At this moment an exceedingly aristocratic motor
car glided into the barn lot through the open gate,
and a thin figure bent over the wheel called, "Hello,
Next Wednesday! What you doing?"

"Hello, Hall," said Next Wednesday. "I pulled
out my defferintial up in ther deadnin', haulin' logs,
an' my exhaust air mixed up 'ith my magneto. I
air now a-puttin' my chassis on ther runnin' gyears.
Want ter git out an' holp?"

Two portly, elderly men, smiling broadly, stepped
down and assisted Peter and Next Wednesday in
lifting the wagon bed on the running gears.

"Murch obleeged, Doc. Murch obleeged, Jedge. I 'm aimin' ter ride over ter Timple's store up at Pleasant Hill, hit bein' er dinged Wednesday."

"Hop in the car, and I 'll drive you over. Plenty of time," said Hall.

"Yeah, but I got comp'ny. They is jist a-roamin' an' lookin at ther kintry. I 'lowed I 'd carry 'em over ter see ther store."

"Get in. Room for everyone in the old bus."

"Traveling in a car?" asked the judge of Peter.

"No, they hain't," said Next Wednesday quickly. "They is seein' ther kintry; which no man kin do in er car. Step over an' see ther Sisyphus. An' thet dawg a-settin' on ther front seat 'ith ye already, Hall, air er human named John."

"Oh, hitch hikers," said Hall. "Catch many rides?"

"No," answered Peter, "walking with a pushcart and a dog is scarcely conducive to catching rides."

"By George! I always did want a walking tour in America," cried Hall. "But you can't walk far a day and push that cart."

"There seems," said Peter, "no especial reason why we should walk far in a day, unless the road is uninteresting."

The three men stared, and, examining Sisyphus curiously, showered us with questions. Next Wednesday had gone for a sack of corn and a kerosene jug. And presently we sank down into luxurious cushions, much to the delight of John, who is something of a snob about cars, and glided away around the mountain to the north.

Odd the certain change of spirit that comes with a swifter pace, and even a slight elevation. The sense of power no doubt repays us for the lost delight of kinship with the earth. But sometimes on dewy summer mornings I have wished that I might dwindle to the height of John, scamper through the wet fields, and share the frantic joy he finds in little earthy things my head is too high to see. The murmuring streams through which the car contemptuously dashes — we cannot hear their pleasant greeting. The wayside trees, past which the motor carelessly sings — they are no more shaded sanctuary where we may rest and meet the birds. Speed. Hours saved for better spending, perhaps. But nymphs and dryads we glimpse no more, and Pan has taken to his heels.

At the summit of a rocky hill Next Wednesday touched Hall's arm and the car stopped. "Her grave," said Next Wednesday. "Dottie's — thar behint ther big pine." And he reverently removed his limp felt hat. Hall glanced curiously at the old man, but looked across at the desolate mound in the high wild grass, and took off his golf cap.

"Drive on, Hall!" cried Dr. Johnson. "That is one grave that makes me want to swear in the presence of ladies!"

"Conscience too tender," smiled the judge. "You can't be expected to save them all."

"Confound you," cried the doctor, "it was n't *my* conscience."

"I reckon, Jedge," said Next Wednesday, "thet ye 'low Doc feels a-passin' er buryin' ground lak ye feels a-passin' er pinertintiary."

And lightly we glided on past the little grave to which no path led.

At Pleasant Hill — a half-dozen houses set back on farms — we stopped a moment by the river with its mossy ruined water wheel and left the "turn o' corn" for the puffing engine of the little gristmill. Then, around the corner, we parked the car before a white painted building, and all walked across the hot, sunny porch into the cool depths of a long room smelling not unpleasantly of brown sugar and smoked meats.

At the left was a little cage built halfway to the ceiling — the post office of Pleasant Hill. Opposite were shelves piled high with snuff cans. Beyond were groceries, dry goods, brooms, hardware, barrels and boxes. In the centre was a fly-specked show case containing paper and envelopes, pins and needles, thread, and summer hats with faded ribbons.

The back door was open, and in the cool breeze behind a huge rusty stove were half a dozen men seated on nail kegs, watching the exciting finish of a checker game.

The proprietor of the store did not look up as we entered. It was his move. Next Wednesday looked carefully at the checker men and said, "Hurry up, Willum. He's got ye beat inyway."

"Want sumpen?" asked the storekeeper absently, frowning over the board on his knees.

"Yeah, I'm in a hurry. Jist fill my coal-oil jug, will ye? I kim in er car an' hed ter carry this hyar leetle jug. Hit'll only hold 'bout half er gallon. Keerful ye don't run hit over."

Mr. Temple rose to his six feet, as straight as an arrow. He was an old man with aristocratic features and a bearing which might have been a direct inheritance from his illustrious forbear. He opened his mouth occasionally to an amazing width as if to laugh, but no sound came. I found this habit so fascinating that I followed them to the back porch for the kerosene.

"Thar! I told ye hit would n't hold no gallon! Ye've spilt hit all over ther place, a-runnin' hit over!" cried Next Wednesday. "How murch do I owe ye, Willum?"

"Wal," said Mr. Temple with a wide picture-laugh, "countin' whut I spilt, an' thet I hev ter go ter ther well ter wash my hands, I reckon I gotter charge ye fur er gallon."

"All right. Kim on in now. I want some o' thim cigarettes. Three er four boxes. I ben smokin' up a feller's thet air a-visitin' me."

"I hain't got but one package. I don't aim ter keep no more. Hit's too murch trouble. Folks is a-wantin' me ter keep so murch stock I hain't no

time ter tind ther post office.   I jist swings back an'
fo'th now twell I don' know whither I 'm handin'
out er man the county paper er a can er snuff."

"Why n't ye git holp, Willum, an' keep iverthing
we all wants ?"

Slowly Mr. Temple's soundless laugh vanished.
"Yeah," he said bitterly, "an' hev ter make
ther holp deppity postmaster an' allers a-buttin'
inter one anither runnin' back an' fo'th frum the
counter ter ther office, an' me hevin' ter go ert
Springdale ter buy goods.   I don't git time 'nuff
now fur a reasonable game o' checkers — only in
crop time."

"May I have a package of envelopes and a pound
of cheese, please ?" I asked apologetically.

"Yas 'm, but thim envelopes hain't no 'count.
They somehow gaums up ther ink on 'em.   But I
got some stamped ones in ther post office.   Thim
cheese air mighty strong an' bitey, but you-all kin
eat some an' see effen ye lak hit."

Our party had found nail kegs behind the rusty
stove into which at certain intervals each man spat,
closing the heavy door carefully for the next man
to open when necessary.   There was an animated
conversation in progress, and I lingered near enough
to listen, but not too close to violate traditional
mountain modesty.   John, who had remained in
the car, barked savagely, and I ran out followed by
Peter and Hall, to find the dog resentfully defending
Hall's car from the too close scrutiny of three boys

on mules. Peter apologized. "John has camped with us so long that he considers any place we stop home."

"I 'd like a dog like that," said Hall. "Want to sell him?"

We made no answer to this obviously absurd question, and returned to the group around the stove.

A long fierce man with jet-black hair and a high intellectual forehead pulled excitedly at the left wing of a raven moustache. "Yeah," he said, "I knows some folks 'lows ther yearth is round. But hit air er lie — though I hain't sayin' they don't believe hit. Ther wust whoopin' I iver got war whin ther school-teacher tried ter make me say thet ther yearth wuz round. I tole him my ole mammy could read, an' miny 's ther time I hearn her read outern ther Bible thet ther yearth hes four corners. Now ye would n't call er squar' field 'ith four corners round, would ye? An' thet settles hit. I allers laid off ter whoop thet teacher whin I growed up. Hit air er quare sarcumstance thet I niver set eyes on him sence!"

"But, Reed," said Dr. Johnson, "men go around the world, you know."

"I claim — not meanin' no harm, Doc — thet hit air er lie. They jist goes round in er circle. Ye cain't git past thim things they calls ther poles. They air high finces er ice ther good Lord putt thar ter keep us frum fallin' off. Sometimes I reckon I 'm ther onliest man in ther world thet 's lift thet

believes ther Bible.   Oncet in er while I gits plumb
lonesome."

There was a moment's silence; no one wished to
wound his spirit further.   A youth with starry eyes
walked slowly to the stove, spat impressively, and
carefully closed the rusty door.   "The thing thet
pesters me a heap," he said, "is whut hit means in
ther Bible whin hit says, 'Time shall be no more.'
Hit do say jist thet!   But whut on yearth 'll take
ther place o' Time whin lak hit says 'Time shall be
no more'?"

The boy stood with his handsome head thrown
back like a deer, awaiting a reply.   But none came.
Each man sat lost in the sublimity of the abyss
suddenly revealed.   And in the awed silence we went
out and got into the car.

At the mill where we stopped for the "turn o'
corn" Hall threw back his head and laughed long
and loud.

"Fancy," he cried, "those chaps sitting behind
that stove solemnly discussing those old fables."

"Yeah," said Next Wednesday, "whin they might
a ben discussin' wither yo' new car body is sufficient
stream-lak, er improvin' ther minds 'bout whut reely
is ther matter 'ith Doc's putts."

"Score one for you, Next Wednesday!" cried the
doctor.

"Now just for that, I 'm going to step on her,"
laughed Hall.   "Someone hold the dog."   And we
rushed home at alarming speed.

"Now," said Next Wednesday, "you-all light an' hitch an' stay fur dinner. Fish an' spoon corn braid outer fraish meal. An' I see mule tracks. Thet means thet Burnis hes brung over Widnesday's yaller Transparent apple pies."

"Hurrah!" cried Hall. "Corn bread without the life ground out of the meal!"

But the doctor looked at his watch and said: "Sorry. Can't let my patients choke down — even for spoon corn bread and Burnis's pie. Sorry, Hall."

"I say," said Hall, "what's the matter with driving out for all of you to-morrow afternoon? Have dinner — supper — with us at the Mansion House and show these people the town."

"I thank you," said Peter, "we should like that. But we start to Wildcat at sunrise to-morrow."

"Wildcat!" cried the doctor. "What for? Wildcat is full of mudholes and idiots! None too safe either — for strangers."

The judge cleared his throat. "Of course this country is perfectly safe anywhere — perfectly. Though we don't pride ourselves on Wildcat Settlement."

"How about selling the dog?" asked Hall. "Name your price. Of course he's not a thoroughbred. Is he trained?"

"No," answered Peter, "he is not a thoroughbred, he is not trained, and he is not for sale."

"Hall," said Next Wednesday, drawing down his

eyes at the corners, "hain't ye larned yit thet thar 's
some things money cain't buy?"

"Yes," said Hall grimly, "it will not buy health.
But it will buy dogs."

"Mebby ye air led inter thinkin' thet John air
tuck up 'ith ye? He jist hain't diskivered the
human race air onnery yit. Whin ye stips on John's
tail he takes hit fur a chancet ter git patted on ther
haid. Effen he war to lose Sister hyar he 'd take
ter drinkin' er tryin' suicidin'."

"He did just that when she went to the infirmary
for three weeks," laughed Peter. "Took the boat
alone across Mobile Bay. Could n't find her.
Came back and went to the dogs completely down
in niggertown."

When the car had disappeared, Peter said:
"What did the doctor mean about the Wildcat
idiots?"

"Thim igits at Wildcat pesters Doc a heap. He
claims they hes all married ther kin an' ther chillern
is lakin'. He 'lows hit air a eugeenical law. But
thar is Boge Whorley — they calls him Boge 'cause
he jist goes boagin' round 'ith no sinse. But
thar 's Mary, his nixt sister, as peart as they
make 'em. An' ole Miss Lawson air plumb 'crazy,
but hit war caused by her babe a-dyin' 'ithout no
doctor — the water bein' high. Though hit air not
right ter let her roam Wildcat an' th'ow rocks at
folks."

My spirits were slightly dampened by this glimpse

of Wildcat; but we dined sumptuously with Next Wednesday and found honey and cream on "yaller Transparent pie" better by far than cheese.

Peter at once set about repairing the wheel of the pushcart. Sisyphus was always stubborn on such occasions, and knowing the difficulty of remaining neutral in the altercation, I said : —

"Shall we go to the river, Next Wednesday? Of course the fish are not biting. But I want to remember my last afternoon by Wanderin' River. Sometimes when the trees are bare, and the ice skims the water, do you find it a bit desolate there?"

"Why, no 'm. Mebby I likes hit best thin. Ye cain't rightly see a tree whin hit 's all dressed up in leaves. Whut I mean is thet the color o' things kinder blinds ye to 'em. Lak a gal 'ith a purty complixion makes ye fergit she 's cross-eyed. Sometimes shadders o' things seem reeler thin ther things theirselves. Oncet I seen er lot o' picters o' big min in ther paper. Jist thar bare haids — sillyhoots, they calls thim picters. Dinged effen I could n't tell more 'bout thim fellers thin whin they wuz all dressed up in hair an' ixprissions! Hit air lak thet by ther river in w'nter. But ye go on down. I 'll kim tereckly. Hit bein' a Widnesday, I got er disagreeble dooty ter perform. I 'll stanter down whin I gits 'em patched."

It was an August afternoon, poised for summer's flight — her wings still furled. Not one red fallen leaf of the sourwood. For the sourwood in the mountains lights the first blazing torch in autumn's sad processional.

Beside the river a spangled butterfly on the golden rim of a trumpet flower rested hesitant in the still drowsy air. Even the iridescent dragon fly darted lazily. The winds slept, but a little truant breeze played sometimes in the willows, too indolent to remain long awake. Beyond the clear green water of the river, the mountains, lilac with the haze of forest fires, melted into the serene sky where great white clouds drifted idly at anchor.

I leaned against a tall gray rock where the passion vine climbed and watched the weaving shadows beyond the quiet water. Near the edge a great cluster of purple ageratum bloomed and there a pompous green frog swelled slowly and enormously. Beyond the willows, on the high sloping bank, I saw feathery water oaks and the perfect lines of tall sweet gums. At the summit stood the haughty, withdrawn pines.

Inevitably beside running-water rhythm — eternal symbol of life — the mind turns sadly to the transience of all life. Millions and millions of little drops obeying blindly a law that leads them ever onward. Dissolved by the sun, lost in the sands, quenching the world's thirst, only the cruel mystery of the sea their goal. Rhythm — and yet the first six bars of a Beethoven symphony, or the single sweep of a master's bow, and all boundaries are erased. No more eternal questioning. All solved in some mysterious way instantly and graphically, and the heart understands that in my father's house are many mansions. But with the rhythm of the river come the baffling thoughts of Time, of Space, of Beauty; the futility of effort in this our orphan world.

I dreamed perhaps. For suddenly I rubbed my eyes and stared across the river. There beyond the willows among the pines was a cabin. It was built of great logs, and through the open door I could see the narrow shelf above the gray rock fireplace. How strange that I had never seen the cabin there. Never. And how many times as I fished I had rested my eyes on the hills beyond the river! Strange, too, that Next Wednesday had never spoken of it; or Peter, who was always interested in anything made by human hands.

It gave no impression of a deserted house. The grass was brown about the cabin, and the space before the door clean-swept. Had I woven a picture of swaying boughs and dense shadows in my dream? But no; when I turned my eyes and looked again it was· always there, brown and mellowed by time, a pathetic little defense against the lonely forest.

Next Wednesday walked briskly down the sloping bank wearing clean faded overalls with a brilliant blue patch on either knee. He had the air of a man who had put duty behind him — as if it might have been already Thursday.

"Why," I said softly, "have we never spoken of the little cabin across the river?"

Next Wednesday sat a little way from me and removed his hat — a most unusual gesture. Then very slowly he said, "Sister, do you see a house across the river?"

"Why, of course. I can see the fireplace through the open door. And a vine climbs by the queer little window. Why, it looks like frost on the vine!"

"Look clost. Do ye see inybody standin' in ther door?"

"A woman is standing there! I did not see her. Look! She is waving her arms. She is calling someone. Do you hear her? I cannot. How her long hair streams in the wind! Why, there is no wind this side of the river." And I turned bewildered eyes to Next Wednesday.

"Look again, Sister. Do you see her now?"

"No, she has gone. And the cabin! It is gone too! Only the pines are there!"

"Ye air ther onliest one excipt me an' one ither thet iver seen thet house an' thet womern. I fust see hit whin I war a leetle lad, an' whin I tole hit I war whooped fur lyin'. I seen hit agin whin I war a growin' boy, an' thin arter I married Viney an' Burnis kim. Not often. Jist sometimes. An' niver since Viney died twell ter-day. I tried secret-lak ter git folks down hyar, an' hyar 'em mintion seein' hit. I niver tole nobody 'bout hit but Mr. Leonard. He dwelt 'ith us fur nigh on ter six yars, an' teached sometimes. I plumb looked up ter Mr. Leonard, though this day I'm tellin' ye 'bout I war most eighteen, an' he war twinty-eight. Hit war a warm day in ther fall o' ther yar, an' he kim down a-leanin' on ther cane I made him. Hit war ther last time afore he died in November. He war a-settin' jist whar ye air now, an' I wuz talkin' 'bout ther house acrost ther river; an' he wuz a-tellin' me 'bout mirages, an' halloonicinations, an' illusions, an' superstitions. But hit seemed lak ther more he explained ther more mixered I got, an' I tole him so. Effen we all hes ter turn iverthing upside down ter see inything, whut turns hit? An' could n't sumpen turn hit over 'ithout thar bein' inything reely thar ter see? He war patient 'ith my ignerance lak he allers war. But he war pow'ful weak an' sad-lak this day. An' he says, 'Bob, I must take a long, long look acrost ther river. Hit 'll be my last dream by Wanderin' River.'

"An' he tuck a long look, an' he seen ther house an' ther womern! An' whin hit faded lak it does, he says, 'Time I wuz settin' sail fur home. Yer mind is the strongest now, Bob.' He died nixt week."

"Did you ever find out if there really was a cabin there once?"

"'Bout five yar ergo over ter ther old settlers' picnic at Laurel-hell Holler Grandpap Grier, — he air ther oldest man in ther mountings, an' kinder wanderin' in his haid, — he war tellin' er crowd 'bout er womern thet hung herself frum ther rafters in er house fur off frum inybody, arter some prowlin' Injuns kilt her man an' carried off her onliest chile.

He hyard ther tale frum his pappy an' hit war somers round 'bout Wanderin' River over by Chicken Bristle settlemint.   He wandered off 'bout ther war he fit in, an' how brave he fit, an' I could n't git him back on ther tale noways.   I hev puzzled a heap 'bout thet yarn.   Ye know ther 's pow'ful quare things in ther papers o' late 'bout Time.   I reads hit — not onderstandin' hit murch.   Tother day a man writ that a stair could plumb die out, an' arter hit hed ben daid a few millions o' yars we all of a suddent could see thet stair.   An' hit 'd be *now* whin we see hit.   Hit air plumb bafflin'.   An' hit 's quare thet ye an' Mr. Leonard air ther onliest ones iver ter see thet house an' womern besides me."

"Peter will say that you heard that tale in early childhood and forgot it — and the whipping fixed it in your mind."

"Hit shore fixed hit!   An' I hain't denyin' imagernation air a pow'ful thing.   Though thim highfalutin ixplanations seems more reedickulous thin ther seein' ther thing.   But I 'low nobody whooped ye an' Mr. Leonard inter seein' hit."

"Oh, he 'd say — mind, *I* don't — that you hypnotized — mesmerized — us.   But I *saw* it.   I saw the cabin and I saw the woman."

"Wal, effen I kin mesmerize ye down by ther river whilst I 'm up at ther house thinkin' 'bout nothin' but ter git thet dinged patch on my britches, I 'low I 'm a marvel!   Speakin' er tellin' Peter, — I don' niver interfere 'ith martial relations, — but me, I hain't niver hed no luck tellin' thet tale. Mebby even Mr. Leonard 'lowed I mesmerized him. Dinged effen I hain't lift my pipe in my ither britches! I 'll run an' git hit. Kin I fotch ye er nip o' blackberry wine an' er piece er pie? Ye looks dauncy — lak ye 'd saw a token."

I told him thankfully that he might. For while I was in no way disturbed by the vision of the cabin, yet a sense of otherwhereness seemed to brood about the river. I had the feeling of one awakened from a vivid dream which awakening did not dispel. A nip and a piece of pie belonged to this accustomed three-dimensional world. For a quiet sense of unreality possessed the place. And when a hollow groan came from behind the rock where I leaned, it too seemed unreal. It was only when there came the sounds of sobs distinctly human that I was minded to creep around the rock to look.

On the grass by the river was stretched a slim figure, incredibly long. A youth lay sobbing, his face in a cluster of blossoming fire pinks, his auburn curls a tousled mat like the fur of a little animal curled there. His thin shoulders under the faded blue of his blouse moved with his sobs like the wings of an imprisoned bird. I crept silently back, and when Next Wednesday appeared smoking contentedly and bearing a covered dish, I motioned him to silence and told him in a whisper of the figure beyond the rock.

"Hit 's Mark Spotswood, I 'low. Hit war jist

this time last yar whin Dottie died. He reckoned
she war pledged ter him. He plumb lost his ree-
leegion whin she died lak she did. I misdoubts he 's
drunk. I 'low I 'm *e*-licted ter say some haish words
ter him — though grievin' fur ther lad. Set still
so 's he won't see yer an' be 'shamed.

"Howdy, Mark. Dinged effen I lak ter stepped
on ye! Hain't seen nothin' er my breachy ole white
cow, hev ye?" No answer. Next Wednesday was
giving the boy time to save his face. I heard him
scratch a match on the rock and seat himself there.

"Hit air er plumb purty place ter sleep hit off —
right hyar aside Wanderin' River. Yeah, I done
jist thet better 'n thirty yar ergo, whin I lays my
haid in thet same bunch er bloomin' fire pinks —
leastways ther great-grandmammy o' thirty yars
back. Hit war jist whin I 'd found out I wuz a
hill-billy pyore an' simple, an' niver would be nothin'
else. A visitin' gal frum Nashville thet I tried ter
dance 'ith assisted me in ther diskivery. Yeah,
ther river an' thim fire pinks kinder holps er man ter
reelize whut a dinged fool he hes ben — an' is."

"Oh, heish up!" cried a shrill anguished voice.
"I wusht I war daid!"

"So 'd I. An' I hain't sayin' I ain't wusht hit
sometimes sence. But so long as I hain't, I ain't
a-wailin' 'bout hit. I 'lows ter play ther man whilst
I 'm hyar — not jist quit work lak some folks, an'
howl lak a dawg whin ther moon shines."

"Effen ye wuz n't a ole man I 'd whoop hell outen

ye fur thim words! I knows how onnery I am an' hit hain't nobody's business but mine. Heish up!"

"Wal, I dunno 'bout thet. Yer mammy thet bore ye an' yer leetle brother Jody — I hyar they hes putt in er crop on corn braid an' sorghum, whilst ye wuz carryin' on over at Wildcat. Hit might, ye might say, be their business."

"Thet air er lie. I sint 'em some money I airned a-playin' siven up. Mammy hated an' despised her thet 's daid. An' I hates an' despises iverbody — frum ye ter ther Presidint o' ther United States! Go on erway an' leave me erlone."

"Yeah. I hearn as how ye air a infi-*del* now, Mark."

"An' ye hearn right. Go on erway. I ain't a-pesterin' ye. I 'm aimin' ter go on ter Wildcat."

"Wal, effen ye air hell-bint an' predetermined ter holp make ther world better by jinin' in 'ith thet low-down crowd over at Wildcat, git up an' light out. Fur effen they hain't no Gawd, er man thet knows hit lak er infi-*del* does, hit 's jist up ter him ter improve the world hisself."

"Holp hell! Ye knows I dreampt o' bein' a preacher an' holpin' ther world. I hain't a-goin' ter holp make folks believe in no Gawd thet 's crueller thin iny man. An' how else kin ye holp er world ixcipt a-savin' ther dad-gasted no-'count souls?"

"'Pears ter me ye is mighty mixed up in yer mind, Mark. An' all fur a gal thet did n't give three whoops fur ye whin she war alive."

"By Gawd, ole man, ye heish! Heish! Er I would n't give three whoops in hell fur yer life!"

"Ca'm down. Ca'm down, Mark. Ye uster hev a brain afore hit war soaked up 'ith red-devil-lye whiskey. Effen ye hain't plumb looney ye knows I 'm ther best frind ye got — an' I war hers, too."

There was a long silence, and I heard Next Wednesday strike a match on the rock.

Then, slowly, the young voice that broke: "Hit air true, Nixt Widnesday. I 'low I am plumb crazy. Whin er feller loses his dreams — ther thing he 's dreampt ter be, an' ter do, an' ther things he 's dreampt war true — he air lak a tumbleweed a-blowin' in ther wind. I 'low I hev committed ther onpardonable sin, an' I air doomed ter hell. I figger thet I 've allers ben lakin'. I 'm goin' ter go way ter furrin places. I ain't no good ter mammy an' Jody nohow. I wusht I knowed whur ter start ter."

"Ther air some folks a-stoppin' in my tree house. They air jist a-roamin'. Ther womern air down by ther river now. Whut say I call her an' axes 'bout thim furrin places an' yer chances?"

"Don't ye do hit! I hates womern. An' her a gypsy womern! I 'low I 'll be goin' on ter Wildcat."

"Nope. Ye hain't goin' ter no Wildcat this night, Mark Spotswood. Lessen hit be over my daid body!" And Next Wednesday called to me as to one afar off. I swallowed hard, offered a silent prayer for Peter to arrive, commended my soul to God, and came from behind the rock. And Heaven forgive me if, in answer to Next Wednesday's adroit questions, I painted too dark a picture of the industrial world beyond the mountains. The youth had given me a sullen "Howdy." His hat lay on the grass by the fire pinks, and he could not retrieve it without rising, so that I saw his marble forehead below the dull red mane of his hair. From his face with the chiseled features of the mountaineer glowed great brown eyes filled with youth's fierce rebellion at the mystery of pain. He listened to our conversation listlessly, but at last said: "I 'low ye air goin' back ter thim places whar livin', fur ther pore, air so hard. I reckon ye hain't aimin' ter stay 'way frum hit. Lincoln, he war a gret man, but he got erway frum thim lonesome places."

"I 'low," said Next Wednesday, "thet Lincoln war not gittin' *erway*. He war goin' *to*. Does yer mind draw ye ter thim places, Mark?"

"I telled ye I hain't got no mind! I air lakin'. Plumb lakin'. I don't know the very littlest thing 'bout my mind. I air er fool!"

"Wal, ye need n't take hit so hard. Ther last thing iny man knows is his own mind. Ther greatest writin' in ther world — barrin' ther Bible — Mr. Leonard claimed war a piece erbout er man thet could n't noways make up his mind. He war er prince an' I allers 'lowed effen he 'd a hed ter cut sprouts instid er jist stanter round an' talk an' think he 'd er got th'ough quicker. But we gotter be plumb thankful he did n't er we would n't er hed ther

piece erbout hit. Now ye take me, fur instant.
'Bout fifteen yar ergo I war thet prideful I thort I
hed figgered out my mind ter a T. I hed plumb
egacted out ther life I meant ter live. I hed give up
all dreams o' gittin' money — only jist 'nuff ter be
easy-lak. But a man hes ter hev dreams. Whin
one goes anither kims. He's made thet-erway.
So I dreampt o' kinder settin' back an' readin' an'
thinkin' an' kinder holpin' ither folks as might want
ter read an' think. Yeah, I hed dag down in my
own mind twell I war plumb contint 'ith whut I
found thar. Thin hit kim! Viney hed ter be operated on. I hed er leetle saved up, an' I sold er cow-
brute er two. Hed jist enough ter git me ter ther
city an' back on the railroad, an' ter pay ther big
city doc, an' ther hosspittle. I knowed I'd hev ter
count iver cint effen iverthing turned out right.
Gawddlemighty! I dasn't think no ither way.
Hit war Viney!

"Dinged effen iver room in thet hosspittle war n't
full o' flowers but Viney's! They war a-settin' out
afore ther doors in ther halls. She hed ter be in er
room 'ith ither folks — not hevin' 'nuff money — an'
nary er flower! 'T would n't troubled some folks
none, but I seen Viney's face fall whin she wint in.
An' me 'ith not 'nuff money ter spar' fur even a leetle
bokay. Fur they sells posies thar, an' 't war late in
the fall o' ther yar.

"I wuz plumb tore up. I clumped up an' down
thim hard sidewalks whin she war bein' operated on,

an' fingered ther money in my pocket an' thort o' buyin' some posies an' settin' out ter walk part-way home arterward — fur I hed ter go back as soon as Viney war called safe. Wal, I clumped erlong afeard ter go back ter ther hosspittle an' afeard not to. Jist as I belongs ter go, thar behint a fine iron gate in er front yard war some o' thim yaller blooms Viney thinks a heap of. Chrysanthems — thet 's hit — as big as cabbage. Gawddlemighty, how I wanted thim posies! Rickolict now I hed ben pridin' mysilf on not makin' money, an' bein' contint 'ith bein' pore.

"Ther road wuz full o' rich folks ridin' by in automobiles, not knowin' erbout Viney ner keerin', an' not er soul ter say, 'She 's in Gawd's hands, Bob.' I plumb hated thim rich folks in ther big house. An' I 'lowed Gawd hisself hed n't no use fur pore folks. Yeah, I wuz plumb tore up. An' all of a suddent I whoops out my knife an' clumb ther iron fince an' cuts er big handful o' thim yaller chrysanthems, an' kivers ther blooms 'ith the paper wropped round my dinner an' th'owed ther vittles erway, an' started on er run fur ther hosspittle. I felt a big hand on my shoulder, an' thar stud er *po*-liceman.

"He says, 'Kim erlong o' me. I seen ye.' I war thet lonesome thet I war, ye might say, eased down by hearin' er man a-speakin' ter me even effen he war arrestin' me. An' 'fore I knowed hit I wuz tellin' him all 'bout Viney bein' operated on an' me wantin' the posies fur her. I wound up a-sayin' plumb desperate-lak, 'Kim on an' take me ter ther jail house. I don't 'mount ter nothin' noways. I might a-knowed ye war a-lookin'.'

"Ther *po*-liceman he drawed hisself up an' he says, 'I ain't a-lookin' now, am I?' An' he turns his back an' stands still. I lets out er whoop an' starts on er run down ther road to ther hosspittle. But ther *po*-liceman he hollers, 'Stop, ye hick!' An' I stopped. He says, 'Shore an' ye 'll git run in yit; a-boundin' an' a-buttin' erlong lak thet!' An' he calls ter a man stoppin' by 'ith er automobile, 'Charley, drive this jay round ter ther infirmary, an' start him ter ther front intrance.'

"I got out at ther hosspittle an' wint up in ther elevator an' runs ter Viney's room whar ther ither sick folks wuz. Viney war a-layin' on ther baid white an' still as death. A nurse war a-settin' by her a-lookin' at her. I knowed she war daid an' I jist drapped down on a cheer froze. Plumb froze. I set thar a-holdin' thim chrysanthems straight out lak I war hevin' my picter tuck. Ther doc he kims in an' the nurse she says, 'She 's coming out of it nicely.' An' the doc says: 'You can go on home, Mr. Cole. It was not malignant.'

"I laid thim posies on ther baid whar she 'd see 'em ther first thing whin she waked up, an' I made fur ther door an' lent agin hit an' cried inter ther handkerchief she 'd ironed so nice fur me an' tole me ter use.

"Yeah, ye jist putt er man in er plumb new envi-*ron*-mint an' no tellin' whut he 'll find hisself a-doin'. In leetle better 'n a hour I 'd clar fergot my rule o' life an' hed envied ther rich, I 'd stole, an' I 'd disbelieved in Gawd.

"Dinged effen hit hain't goin' ter storm! An' Link an' Burnis war a-comin' over ter-night. Mark, ye kim on home 'ith me an' git in ther dry wood whilst I does up ther chores. Hit air the first cold August rain a-comin'. We 'll all eat supper an' thin we 'll go inter Mr. Leonard's room an' Sister hyar, mebby she 'll read out loud ther story o' ther man thet hed er heap o' trouble makin' up his mind."

Suddenly I shivered with the chill wind from the river, and looking up saw black pirate clouds chasing the white sails from the sky.

We found Peter, John, and Sisyphus already established in the house, and Peter building a fire in the kitchen.

After supper, while the flames flickered on the white walls of Mr. Leonard's room, I sat in the rustic easy-chair beside the rosy lamp shade and read.

Peter lay on the goatskin before the fire with John beside him. Next Wednesday sat in the chimney corner renewing his pipe with the live coals and hearing, I knew, another voice than mine. The youth perched perilously on the edge of his chair, one long leg wrapped about the round, his thin arms dangling, his great bewildered eyes fixed upon me.

And while the thunder growled, retreated, and came again, and the rain drummed on the roof of the lonely mountain cabin, I read aloud the immortal words of Hamlet: Prince of Denmark.

XIII

WILDCAT SETTLEMENT

In the false dawn, soft *madrugada* of the Spanish, we very quietly pushed Sisyphus through the dark dog-trot, whispered John to silence, and under the morning stars set out to Wildcat.

Our visit with Next Wednesday had closed at midnight on such a full, satisfying chord of comradeship that we dreaded a casual note in the music of memory. So we stayed for no farewell. Only a penciled line left on the kitchen table, and two small volumes of essays we happened to have with us — one inscribed to our dear Next Wednesday, and one to the boy, Mark Spotswood.

We walked softly under the clear song of the stars. For it is the morning stars that sing together. In lonely mountain camps we never hear the night stars sing. Perhaps our ears are dulled by the clamor of the day. They seem very far away, silent with the resignation of faith — or of despair. And now, the earth washed sweet by last night's rain, the wet leaves trembled with the nearness of dawn.

John, frantic with joy at the open road once more, disappeared in the shadows of the deep wood, and Sisyphus rattled happily over the rain-sharpened rocks.

"This constant breaking of home ties!" cried Peter. "We grow attached at the slightest opportunity. Say we camp alone after this."

"Oh, but that is being afraid of life, is n't it?"

"According to report, there are idiots and mudholes to be afraid of to-day. And the most sumptuous still in the mountains. The fellow who runs it is king of Wildcat Settlement. I left John's harness out for the mudholes."

John knew it. He always knew. He would return when the way grew difficult and pull cheerfully as we urged Sis over some steep bank, or through deep mud where his four feet trotted lightly.

The dawn breeze died. The last star faded. And as the light suffused the dense wood that surrounded us, we stopped on a hilltop overlooking the lush green plateau, watched with never-failing awe the sunrise, and lighted the little flame of our breakfast fire. Water for coffee by the roadside. For every despairing stream was chuckling now, and every drooping mountain flower was smiling with the recent rain.

This day we did not linger for accustomed cigarettes and conversation; for beyond, across the low, level stretch of Wildcat, slept Shady Cove, which we hoped to reach by sunset.

At the base of the mountain we slackened our pace and all three went into harness; for now each foot must be lifted with effort in the thick sticky mud. Once, at a rushing stream with high banks, it took some time and some work to induce Sisyphus to cross on the two frail planks that bridged the swollen creek. And I, who can never walk steadily in high places, shuddered at the foaming depth below.

Noon — and we were at trouble to find a mound dry enough for a comfortable camp, hemmed in as we were by tall dark-shadowed woods of oak and gum and of sycamore and hickory, with fern and spongy moss beneath.

Immediately after a buffet lunch beside Sis we hastened on, although we were undeniably weary, and John so tired we set him free. But we were anxious to finish this journey across Wildcat which abounded, we had been warned, with congenital idiots from intermarriage with "kin," with treacherous mudholes, and with lawless moonshiners.

We had seen several cabins set back in the forest, but now that we were apparently near the centre of the plateau we came upon a rather pretentious log house, and near it a barn three times the size of the house. Something common enough elsewhere, but unusual in the mountains. We picked our way gingerly, the swamps on either side of the road recalling alligators to me and suggesting water moccasins to Peter and John. As we neared the place we could see that there was a corral of oak poles between the barn and the house. It must have been seven feet high, and there appeared to be something exciting taking place within. For on the top rail were perched a dozen men in a row, like so many outlandish birds with half-spread wings. They were squawking wildly: "Now 's yer time! Git 'er now! Look out, Lureely!"

John ran forward and stood transfixed, stiff-legged, staring between the poles of the fence. At this each bird turned his head like an owl and sent us an appraising glance of hostility. An owl hoot of "who-who" would have been more reassuring than this inimical silence. Unabashed, we climbed the fence and augmented the number of birds by two.

Inside the long corral, deep in the mire, at least twenty cows were plunging wildly about. A man with a coil of heavy rope stood in the middle of the enclosure trying, we could see, unsuccessfully to lasso one particular cow who had seen the hand of Fate, for she ran around the outside of the circle of cattle pawing and bellowing.

Time after time the man threw his rope, but the cow always evaded it and plunged about until the whole herd was milling. Deep in the mire a woman with great bare feet splashed about. She wore a long blue calico dress so plastered with mud that it

flapped heavily about her tall thin form. Her sunbonnet had fallen in the mud and her long graying
hair whipped in the wind as she bounded around
calling, "Soo! Soo! Soo, Reddy!" She was carrying a heavy bucket and was endeavoring to place
handfuls of salt on the backs of the frightened cows
in the hope of quieting them when they stopped to
lick the salt from each other's and their own backs.
The foam from their licking lips filled the air like
spindrift in an ocean storm, but they never ceased
to mill. A tall bearded man in high-topped boots
called continually: "Lureely. Kim on outern thar!
Lureely. Let thet air fool man ketch ther consarned
cow-brute. I don't keer effen he don't buy her.
Kim outern thet, Lureely! Ye 'll git trompled!"

It might be supposed that one of the dozen men
who decorated the fence would have gone to the
woman's assistance. But in the mountains a cow is
peculiarly a woman's charge. The man buys and
sells. But no mountain man would so demean himself as to feed or milk a cow; and I have seen cows
frightened by the mere presence of a man. A woman
manages all cows and her interest only expires when
the cow is sold. Now there is the glory of a frenzied
horse, and the grandeur of a maddened bull, but a
cow, when she forgets her dignity and ceases to pose
for her picture beneath a tree or knee-deep in quiet
water, is undeniably an absurd creature. A matron,
fashioned for contented repose in home surroundings,
when she takes on speed her every move is some

grotesque and lumbering antic. It was impossible not to laugh; but I cried to Peter: —

"The poor woman! Why does n't Lureely come out? Why does n't someone go in and help her?"

"Why, yes," said Peter. And to my consternation he dropped lightly from the fence, threw me his sombrero, dodged the racing cattle, and called to the man inside to throw him the rope. There was a high stump in the centre of the corral and Peter, mounting this, cried: "I 'll rope this cow for you; but I want you to understand the moment I have roped her I 'm over the fence and out. It 's up to you then. You can snub her around this stump." No one spoke, and I called involuntarily: "Lureely! Come on out!" But the misguided woman stood staring at Peter, who had spoken as one having authority; and the man brought the rope without a word.

"This is a cable, not a rope," cried Peter. "But I 'll try it." And he stepped from the stump and carefully examined and coiled the rope.

My heart was in my mouth. What utter recklessness! This desperado mood of Peter's would draw down upon us contempt. Already there was hostility. And this, we knew, was the home of the great moonshiner — the king of Wildcat. And the danger! The cows were now tearing about in a way that defies description. And Peter, his black curls flying above his scarlet neckerchief, so very slender compared to these stalwart men of the mountains.

I called to John, fearing he might rush to Peter's assistance and further enrage those terrible animals. But John did not answer. He was waving his white plumed tail in pride and expectancy. His god was adequate to any situation. Of course I knew that Peter had spent some time on a Western dude ranch, but he had never claimed proficiency in roping cattle. Now, astonishingly, unerringly, the heavy rope swirled through the air and dropped precisely over the head of the unfortunate cow in question. In a second Peter was laughing on the fence beside me.

Inside the corral it was no laughing matter. The man had seized the end of the rope and had snubbed it around the stump. But the rope was long and the lassoed cow began to race around the outside of the circle of milling cows, and the screaming woman, as well as the trampling herd, was pressed to the middle of the corral about the stump. Round and round the roped cow ran, gathering the woman and the plunging cattle into a clashing bellowing mass. I shut my eyes, but opened them when a great shout went up. For the bearded man, seizing a rail from the fence, ran into the corral and laid about him valiantly. At last the poor cow fell, and Lureely, unexpectedly alive, limped away toward the house.

A man assisted the buyer with the cow, and the poor creature was dragged from the corral. As he passed us the buyer said : —

"I 'd give a hundred dollars effen I could rope a

cow lak thet! Hit wuz a plumb surprisin' sight on yearth!"

Peter dismissed this praise with a wave of the hand, as if he roped a cow daily before breakfast. But meeting my gaze of awe and pride, he said: "Surprisin' to me too. A long time since I twirled a rope. I wanted to help the old woman; and, by George, I nearly finished her."

Said the buyer to the bearded man: "Hed I knowed thet air cow-brute would a sulled lak thet, I 'd niver bought her. Effen ye iver fish my hat outern thet mud jest give hit to yer womern. She shore airned hit."

Said the bearded man to the buyer: "Hed I knowed whut kind o' a cowman ye air, I would n't a sold her. Effen I iver fish inything outern thet air mud hit 'll be my womern's toenails! Lak 'nuff she air crippled fur life."

Delightedly we called the fascinated and reluctant John and pushed on. The bearded man seemed to be in conference with the men who had sat on the fence. Suddenly he called:—

"Hyar, ye-all. Stop. Ye feller thet roped ther cow — stop!"

We stopped.

"Whar ye aim ter go?"

We replied that we were aiming to go to Shady Cove.

"Got kin thar?"

"No."

"Wal, I 'low ye cain't make hit ter-night. Ye kim inter ther house an' stop by all night. In ther mornin' some o' ther boys 'll show you-all ther short road ter Shady."

The king of Wildcat spoke more in command than in invitation, more in menace than in hospitality. Our eyes met, and we turned and followed him into the house. For always we bore in mind the advice of friendly mountaineers. And when the owner of a still said turn, we turned. And, after all, we had wasted so much time that we knew we should never reach Shady Cove by sunset. So, as Peter whispered, "It 'd not miss-putt us."

Inside the big bare room redolent of muscadine jelly in the making, Peter prevailed upon Lureely to remove the muddy rags from her lacerated feet and to apply antiseptic gauze and peroxide from our little medicine chest. She rewarded us by a sight of her marvelous quilts — her treasure — and by addressing Peter as Doc and informing the household that he "war a Doc." There were three handsome young women, and one beautiful girl of eighteen perhaps, evidently "lakin'." She followed me about, gazing sweetly at me with great blue eyes, fingering my dress, and patting my hand. An innocent.

At an earlier supper than is common among farmers, eight men sat sullenly and silently with us, waited on by the women. When we had finished and were taking snuff — the wine and walnuts of a mountain dinner — one of the women lighted a

lamp and showed us our room, destitute of furniture
but for four beds, one in each corner.

"You-all," she said, "kin pick out whutiver baid ye
want ter. The rest kin take whut 's lift."

We asked permission to bring Sisyphus in and to
tie John to the wheel; and selecting a bed near the
only window that could be raised sank gratefully
into the feathers and awaited the others. Presently
six men with rifles stalked in and, depositing their
firearms beside their beds, blew out the lamp, and
soon the heavy liquor-laden air was filled with snores.

Peter whispered: "Go to sleep. We are safer
here than we should be in camp."

"Of course," I answered in a resigned whisper,
"though they probably mean to shoot us at sunrise."
And we slept sweetly until the sound of the breakfast horn awakened us. The six roommates were
washing their faces at a trough and combing their
respective hairs with a small horn comb hanging by
a long string to the porch wall. They were fine,
fair, strapping young fellows, silent and sullen.
From the bank behind the house by the lazy river
the steam of the still rose gallant and unashamed.

At snuff time the king of Wildcat said curtly,
"Three o' ther boys is goin' yore way." And they
did — one preceding us with his rifle on his shoulder,
and two following, also armed. We marched on
until well past the road that leads from Shady Cove
to the world. Then, telling us the road led straight
from there to the Cove, they left us.

It was an untold relief to shake off the espionage
of this stalking guard, and we trudged on happily,
John picking a better way through the forest and
joining us at intervals.

We passed several small cabins, often guarded by
a moat and a drawbridge of planks. For there were
standing pools of water everywhere, and the rising
steam in the hot August sun made our walking a
perpetual Turkish bath.

Before one of these log cabins we stopped on a
slight elevation to catch the fitful breeze and to rest.
A wild figure in a dress of coarse sacking came running down the path from the house, stopping to reach
for a stone.

"Stop!" she screamed. "Stop, you-all!" And a
rock whizzed through the air, striking Sisyphus with
such force that the scar remains to this day. Peter
quickly pushed me down behind the cart, and running to the woman seized her hands.

"You know," he said quietly, "you must n't do
that."

"I wants my fortune told," croaked the woman.
"Ye air gypsies. I know 'bout gypsies. I wants
my fortune told!"

"We are not fortune tellers," Peter replied, and
released her hands. Instantly she hurled a rock at
me where I had risen and was standing behind Sisyphus. "Ye gotter tell my fortune! I wants my
fortune told!" And suddenly she began to cry.
A pathetic, a terrifying creature. Incredibly emaci-

ated, her head shaven, her immense eyes, blazing
like a light from out an empty skull, peered out as if
all the life in her body had been sucked up by some
alien tenant who gazed out with a wild curiosity at
the world of men. Her hands, which could so well
cast a stone, were great dirty claws. And her
cracked voice was like the croak of some huge threatening bird. From her waist dangled a small rope
that seemed to have been gnawed apart.

Peter, not daring to release her, called repeatedly,
hoping to bring someone from the cabin or the field.
But no answer came. Gently he tried to induce the
woman to return to the house. But at this she
began to fight and to scream. "She's gotter tell
my fortune! I hain't goin' back. I know 'bout
gypsies. I kin read. I wants ter git erway frum
Wildcat! I wants my fortune telled!"

"All right," said Peter desperately, "I 'll tell your
fortune." The demented woman struck at his face
with her long brown claw. "I don't want no man
ter tell my fortune! Hit 's gypsy womern thet tells
fortunes. They looks in yer hand. Tell my fortune, gypsy womern!" She sprang away from
Peter and grasped my hand.

Heaven forgive me if the mere outward appearance
of any human creature should bar me from fellow-
ship in a mad world. But rather would I have faced
the rifle of any moonshiner in Wildcat Settlement
than to have held the hand of this shell of a woman
possessed of a devil. But Peter had reached for

my free hand and was whispering: "Try. If you can."

So I swallowed hard and managed to say, "Sit here on the fallen tree and be very quiet, and I will tell your fortune."

Poor creature! Her fortune! Fortune! The very word filled my mouth with bitterness; signaled the curtain to rise on the farce of life. Each of us on his precarious island of security, cold with a secret fear of the awful acquiescence of the stars. Always the cruel persistence of our dreams amid sardonic laughter of whatever gods there be. Her fortune!

At last the piteous creature seated herself on the wet ground beside the fallen tree and commenced to simper in a silly, satisfied way. I was so overwhelmed with compassion and with horror that I could scarcely stammer the words.

"You are soon to go away from Wildcat," I faltered. "You will go where it is sweet, and cool, and pleasant always — and you will be happy."

"Be whut?" whispered the woman.

"You will be young again, and you will run about as you used to do when your beautiful hair was brown and your cheeks like red roses. You remember a time like that? You will fly as free as a bird wherever you like. This day will only come back to you like the memory of a troubled dream. You will love everyone and everyone will love you."

"Will I hev a pair o' gold yearrings? I allers wanted gold yearrings. Allers I craved 'em."

And oh, the shabby dreams, the gewgaw ambitions that never die! "Yes," I answered firmly, "if you still want them you will have them."

The woman fixed her great eyes on the distant horizon of purple hills and spoke as if to herself. "He allers said he'd git 'em fur me sometime. 'Mammy,' he'd say, 'whin my leetle calf grows up I'll sell hit an' buy ye some gold yearrings.'"

Suddenly the skeleton figure rocked and wept. "I don't want thim yearrings, gypsy womern! Hit hain't thet I wants ye ter tell. I wants him! Thet nice place whar I'm goin' ter, will he be thar? I wants ter hyar him trompin' round in his leetle new boots! I wants ter hyar him sayin' whin I war plumb tired: 'Mammy, I'll holp ye tote ther water frum ther spring in my leetle gourd.' I wants ter hyar him! Hit air so still hyar in Wildcat! Folks dies by tharsilves hyar. Will he be thar too, gypsy womern, in thet nice place whar I'm a-goin'?"

The woman was quiet now and spoke with piteous expectant appeal. Peter turned away his face. For we both knew the sudden silence that comes over the world, never again in its entirety to be lifted. "Tell her!" whispered Peter gently but relentlessly. "Tell her."

And oh, with more assurance than I felt, I answered : —

"Yes, you will have that too: the same voice; the sound of the little feet; and the small hand shut in your own."

The woman looked up through happy tears.

Suddenly we seemed to have drawn all the latent forces of horror that lurk about us into an epitome of all human rebellion and despair. How paltry all our egoistic writhings in a tiny point of time — in a swinging universe. It was grotesque. A demented old woman, two obscure wanderers, and a dog with the ache of dumbness in his throat. The melancholy hills hemming us in here in this remote lost valley.

"Hyar, Miss Annie! Ye leave thim folks erlone, na' kim back ter the house!" called a woman who came running from around the cabin. "She war worser ter-day, an' whin I wint ter ther field I hed ter tie her ter ther baidpost, fearin' she 'd git ter ther branch. She allers makes fur ther water. She air outern her haid sence her boy died an' the water wuz too high fur a doctor ter kim. But hit would n't a done no good noways. He war bited by a moccasin snake. Kim on in now, Miss Annie," said the woman kindly.

"Come on, poor gypsy woman," said Peter. "You 've had an evil dream. We 'll make camp to rest, and I 'll brew you a fine cup of tea."

Easier said than done. For on either side of the road was a swamp, and not until we had come to a wide shallow stream where a great, flat, sun-baked rock lay in the middle of the river was the problem of a camp solved. John, as he often did, suggested the solution. For at once he swam across to the dry island rock, and shaking himself frenziedly stretched out to dry in the sun.

So we unlocked the cart, found our bathing suits, carried Sis across, and soon had a fire blazing on the rock from the débris we found there. It was a happy little river. The water crystal clear, and the banks bordered with laurel and shaded by willows. Presently we were smiling, a trifle wanly perhaps, over our adventures in Wildcat.

"There are those," said Peter, "who might consider Wildcat Settlement an unusual choice for a somewhat belated wedding journey."

"But there's Shady Cove just ahead. And it is better than seasickness or a summer hotel where all is vanity and vexation of spirit."

And, unusually weary, I lay back in the hot sunshine with John beside me, while Peter packed the cart after lunch. For even in this sweet spot we dared not linger to-day. Suddenly Peter whispered : "Lie still. Don't move. There is a man with a rifle hid in the willows behind you." Then — "Hello, stranger. Come across and have a cup of tea with us."

The man lowered his rifle and came through the laurel.

"I'm a-looking fur a wild hawg. Hain't seen none erbout, hev ye?"

"No," said Peter. "Going to shoot him?"

"Wal, I shoots wild hawgs and ither varmints some days. Most mistuck ye-all fur varmints in thim striped clothes."

"Oh," I said, "these are our swimming clothes. Our others are in the cart. Have you had your dinner? We have eaten, but there's some left. Come across."

"No, I ain't ben ter dinner; but I hain't no striped swimmin' clo'es, an' I don't 'low ter git wet. I got ther rheumatiz pow'ful bad."

"I'll wade across and bring you a bucket of tea and a sandwich." And Peter cut two huge slices of bread and two pieces of boiled ham. The man ate and drank eagerly. "Whar ye-all aimin' ter go?" he asked. "Shady Cove," answered Peter. "We spent the night with Sanford."

"Wal, hit hain't nothin' ter be proud of — stayin' 'ith Sanford. Got kin in Shady?"

"No."

"See Sanford's store?"

"No."

"Hit's er big store. I 'low he's got duebills on ther hull settlemint. Nobody hain't got nothin' lift but iniquity in the *en*-tire settlemint."

"Iniquity?" I queried.

"Yeah. He's got a mortgage on iverbody. I hain't got no iniquity lift now myself."

One might suppose that the sudden confidences of the mountaineers are premature. But the customs of sophistication do not obtain in remote places. Reserved, silent, even sullen, when the mountain man condescends to speech with a stranger it is of vital, fundamental things.

"Much obleeged," said the old man as Peter waded across for the cup and plate. "Hit tasted pow'ful good. We air outern meat at our house. I war tryin' ter shoot a wild hawg. I air got ther rheumatiz so bad I cain't work murch. But I gotter new medicine thet holps some." And he unfolded with pride a paper from his pocket and read with great *empressement*.

"Hit air called Blessed Relief; an' ther *di*-rictions says, 'Rub on ther afflicted part in ther mornin' an' before goin' ter baid at night. Keep ther feet dry, an' eat sparin'ly o' meat.' I follers thet last *di*-riction an' all ther fambly follers hit too, I 'lows. Thim *di*-rictions is all right, only I hain't got no parts. I air all afflicted parts. Effen er man kin git his rheumatiz lo-*ca*ted he air placed so he kin work on hisself. Trouble is ter git hit lo-*ca*ted."

To make amicable conversation while Peter packed the cart, I said: "Did you ever try the sun cure? This sun-baked old rock has taken away all the pain in my back."

"Hey?" said the old man. "Mebby so."

"But where," said Peter, "is that fine new pound of butter? It was unusually good butter. I spread the sandwiches with it only a moment ago. It is humanly impossible that it should have disappeared from this rock."

"I 'low the dawg et hit," suggested the old man.

But this I denied. John is an honest dog.

At last, pitying Peter's bewildered state, I arose lazily and assisted in the search.

"He, he, he!" laughed the man. "I reckon I see thet pound o' butter. I 'low hit war not ther rock but ther grease thet holped yer rheumatiz! Hit air stickin' ter ther afflicted part." It was. I must have slid over on it when the man appeared and startled me.

The old man, still chuckling, shouldered his rifle and crept through the laurel. "Effen you-all sees iny wild hawgs jist skeer 'em this-away, will ye? Hit 's er long ways ter Shady. 'Low ye 'll be startin' on in yer clo'es. Apply ter ther afflicted part! He, he, he!"

"He is not hunting hawgs. He is a spy. If we ever get out of Wildcat I would n't cross it again even in an airship."

"Another escape. It is lucky for us he was hungry. Well," said I, speaking without knowledge, "we shall soon be at the Cove. We 'll hurry."

Carrying Sisyphus across the river and changing to our clothes that looked less like "striped varmints," we trudged on through the mire. But where the river made a horseshoe bend there was a small bridge, and across it came a wagon drawn by mules. A man and a woman sat on the spring seat. The mules took fright before we could extricate Sis from the mud and climb the high bank, and the man was at trouble to hold them. The woman pushed back her sunbonnet and cursed us with astounding fluency and vigor. Never before in the mountains had we heard a profane word. Men in the mountains do not swear before their women.

"Ye ort ter be putt offen ther road, skeerin' folks an' takin' up ther road!" She turned her head to some louts leaning on the railing of the bridge and screamed: "Whoop 'em, boys! Whoop 'em outern ther settlemint! The —" And here followed such a minute and vivid description of each of us, of John, and of Sis, that we were compelled to laugh; though I put John on his chain and took the rifle from Sis's slandered back and carried it across the bridge.   One of the youths called, "Whar 'd ye steal thet dawg?" and threw a clod at John.

We felt we had had a narrow escape. And we did not release John nor relax a certain vigilance for an hour. But now we realized with a kind of terror that, owing to our slow progress through the mud, we must make camp. We could not reach Shady Cove by dark. At last we found a mound that seemed high and dry above the swamps, and we set about at once collecting wood for a friendship fire as well as a cooking fire. For already the damp air was rising from the swamp and mosquitoes were singing.

Not until we had established ourselves comfortably did we miss John. I sounded the little whistle we carried, but no white form came bounding through the trees. We were not yet disturbed, for often John disappeared bent on original research, and we would find him farther along waiting to welcome us. So we walked on, searched the woods, and, now thoroughly alarmed, called until it was so dark we feared to lose our way and fall into some treacherous bog. We built a great friendship fire, after our brave attempt at supper, and Peter piled wood near it for what he knew would be for me a sleepless night. Then he set the smudge fire across the door of the tent, and though he insisted that he share the watch with me, I refused the sacrifice. Presently he was asleep in the tent and I was sitting with my back against a tree, staring into the flames, and all about me the cold malice of the night.

Always I have envied Peter, Napoleon, and the entire negro race their ability to advance determinedly into the ocean of sleep. For me, I must climb cliffs, descend tortuous paths, and then fall into slumber by mere accident.

We had exchanged few words as to John's fate. Our hearts were too sick. But we agreed to start back at daylight and search Wildcat Settlement until we found him if we spent the remainder of the summer here.

At intervals, above the mighty chorus of the frogs, I sounded the shrill whistle. And always, as if it had been the signal for the curtain to rise at the theatre, the orchestra was suddenly hushed, and I could hear the whisper of leaves and the crackle of the fire. What a deafening chorus! So many frogs — were they to advance upon us they must bury us tent and all. I had n't thought there were so many frogs in the world!

There was a curious harmony in the pandemonium. As if the deep embedded rocks, the roots of giant trees, the hollow caves inside the earth, gave tongue together in a horrid sanction to the eternal sovereignty of the powers of darkness. There was no mockery, no rebellion in their shouting. Rather a solemn assent to the cruelty that lurks below the flowered surface of their world. Had John slept here with his head on my knee we might have thought it funny — this wild chorus of mournful demons. For listening through the long hours of the night I came to distinguish certain voices. Boom! boom! boom! the mighty bass. A silence — then the lyric soprano trilling away, and waiting an instant for the barytone — then all the voices in triumphant unison.

And ever my mind runs in a vicious circle. He is trapped. He calls us who have never failed him before. Our comrade! He is stolen. He is beaten. John, who has never heard a harsh word. And I scorned myself for wasting such grief upon a dog. Why, there are children in the world to-night beaten, suffering, orphaned, alone. It was useless. My mind would go back to the days when he was a little white fluffy ball, so wildly proud in that hour when he could first jump as high as my couch where I lay ill. And the day when he staggered home, poisoned. And he lay under the chinaberry tree on the cool grass, and Peter said: "Come away. We have done all we can. He is gone." And I leaned down and said, "Good-bye, little friend," and he gave the slightest wag of his plumed tail, and I ran for the cup of hot coffee — and he lived!

They tell us we love dogs because they flatter our vanity — parasitical sycophants. Though John admired Peter extravagantly, one could see that he considered me inferior in all that goes to make a man. And now the memory of those pleading eyes when sometimes I denied him a place in the car — a day that would have meant unalloyed bliss to him — only for the reason that he might cause me some slight inconvenience. We recognized that our friend was not as intelligent as some other dogs we knew. But who loves his friends for their intellectual superiority? John is honest, faithful, brave, and has a real appreciation of beauty — though I hereby proclaim myself a sentimental nature fakir. How loud the frogs sing! Louder. Louder. An indistinguishable ringing in my ears. And day is breaking, and I lie in a crumpled heap by the ashes with a pillow under my head, and a blanket carefully tucked about me.

We made our coffee on the embers of the friendship fire and, hiding Sisyphus in a laurel thicket, set out on the back trail with heavy hearts. But Heaven sent us luck. Behind us trotted two sleek horses, with a wagon driven by a friendly man who asked us if we wanted a lift. We told him our story as we jolted along. He was from Shady Cove and was going "outside for Granny who war over ter Jim Blake's." "No," he said, "you-all's dawg hain't trapped. Thar hain't no trappin' in Wildcat nohow. Nothin' but makin' pore liquor an' sellin' hit, an' raisin' houn' dawgs an' sellin' 'em. Wildcat sells iverthing an' lives as hard as heck. We-all don't neighbor 'ith Wildcat."

"How," asked Peter, "did Wildcat get that way?"

"I kin riccollict back whin Wildcat war as good er settlemint as thar war in these hyar mountings. But whin Sanford got ter sellin' red-devil-lye liquor outside, iverbody got ter makin' hit an' sellin' hit too. Thin Sanford he buys 'em out er whoops 'em outern ther settlemint, an' they loses ther places, an' iverbody loses heart. Why, some o' 'em don't farm a-tall — don't raise nothin'. Effen ther womern did n't make gyarden they 'd starve."

"Here!" I cried, "is the place where I saw John last. He ran east, chasing a rabbit."

"You all jis' project round," said the man, "an' ye 'll find him tied up summers. Ther air some houses back thar up thet road to ther left. I 'll be comin' erlong 'ith Granny this evenin' 'bout four o'clock. I 'll pick ye up on ther road an' ride ye inter Shady. I air ther storekeeper thar, an' ther best campin' spot in ther Cove air jist ter one side o' my store. Git erlong, hosses!" And our only friend in Wildcat was gone.

"How do I projict round?" asked Peter. "I don't know how to projict."

"Neither do I. But I'll carry the rifle and you go ahead and projict."

We came upon a desolate cabin set far back in trees.

"Now," said Peter, "I'll just go in and ask if they've seen our dog. I'm no diploma⁺."

A grim woman with a locked face came to the door and asked us in. "No," she replied to Peter's question, "hit's all we kin do ter take keer o' our own dawgs, 'thout keepin' track o' yourn."

Peter, for a chance to look about, asked if he could get him a fresh drink of water. The woman took the bucket and gourd and said she would go with him to the spring.

By the one window of the room sat an old woman in a clean calico dress. She was piecing a quilt of such a pretty and intricate pattern that I examined the work and told her how beautiful I thought it. She seemed pleased, and showed me all the pieces in her basket. As I followed Peter and the woman out the door, the old woman coughed. There was something significant, portentous in that cough, and I looked back. She beckoned me. "I'll wait here and rest," I called to Peter.

"Now," whispered the old woman, "effen ye'll swar on a stack o' Bibles higher 'n yore haid thet ye won't tell, I'll tell ye sumpen."

I swore.

"Yistiddy evenin' thar war a white dawg runned past hyar — chasin' er varmint, I 'low. I hearn him barkin' over to Al Grier's house nixt ourn. Thin I heerd a dawg howl lak he war ketched an' drug. Minnie, hyar, war outen ther gyarden patch. She musta knowed hit too, but she don't 'low ter hev no trouble 'ith thim Griers. They is low-down folks. I 'low you-all's dawg is shet up thar this holy minute."

"But oh, how can we get him? There are no officers of the law in Wildcat, I suppose. They may not give him up to us."

"Lawsy, no! They aims ter sell him outside. But I 'low ye hes a chancet ter git him effen ye is slick enough. Al Grier an' his biggest boy rid by goin' ter Sanford's airly this mornin'. I hain't seen him kim back. They did n't hev ther dawg, fur I watched 'em. He air a widder man, an' ther won't be nobody home but Solomon. Solly air lackin', but he air plumb stout an' kin fight, though they don't give him no gun. Mostly he air sleepin' under a tree whin his pappy air away. Don't ye let on whin yer man kims 'ith the water. Minnie air my son's womern."

I took from my pocket an envelope containing two bright little handkerchiefs and gave them to the dear old woman.

"Lawsy!" she cried, "thim air too leetle to do no good fur hankerchers. I 'll jis' snip 'em up fur quilt pieces 'fore Minnie gits 'em." And she snipped

them with her great shears and hid them in her
basket.

Catching Peter's eye as he gave me a gourd of
water, I nodded significantly. We thanked the
sullen Minnie and the gallant old woman and went
down the grassy road that led to Grier's.

"What luck!" cried Peter excitedly. "I 'll go
on and climb the side fence. Give me the rifle.
Wait here till I signal you to come. We 'd best be
together. But don't call or whistle if you hear John
howl."

Peter disappeared around the cabin, and in a
minute that seemed an hour he waved to me, and I
climbed the rail fence and joined him at a ruined
barn behind the house.

"My word, but he 's a whale — that Solomon!
He 's asleep on the grass at the east side of the house.
John is not inside. I looked in." Neither was he
in the barn. Oh, could they have sold him outside
already — taken him where we could never find him?
Peter went to look in a henhouse and I turned to a
small shed with the upper half of a locked door open.
I found a piece of plank and climbed up to look
inside. There lay John exhausted, his weary head
between his paws, tied by a thick rope to some
implement. I crept away and brought Peter, then
climbed through the upper door, leaving Peter on
guard with the rifle. I put my hand over John's
mouth and his excited barks changed to sneezes.
But he jumped about so wildly that I could not untie

the rope and had to get Peter's knife to cut it —
horribly frightened at the delay.

At last John vaulted through the door and whined
with his head on Peter's shoulder. I found a keg
and climbed out. We put the chain on John and
ran for the fence, Peter and John in the lead. But
my skirt caught on the fence and I could not tear it
loose. A gigantic, shambling figure came from
behind the cabin and sniffed the air like some huge
wild beast. I screamed to Peter, brought the top
rail down with me, but freed my skirt, and ran for
my life. Forsaking the road, we plunged into the
deep woods. As we cautiously emerged again into
the open road, there, driving down the road from
the north, came two men in a wagon. The Griers!
Laughing hysterically, we all three took to the woods
again until we were almost at the laurel hell where
Sisyphus waited. We pushed on at once and it was
long past noon when we stopped for lunch. But oh,
the delight of that dinner of herbs together!

At last came the rattle of a wagon and our friend
from Shady called: "Got him! Git in. Best putt
him in too so thar won't be no chancet fur a ruckus.
Granny likes dawgs."

How happily we jolted along on the board set
across the wagon for a seat! Peter, John, Sisyphus,
and I. And how gratefully and amiably we clutched
the little bumping interfering form.

"Where is that place called Wildcat?" grinned
Peter. The man turned alarmed eyes, and I

hastened to say, "He means we have forgotten our troubles at Wildcat." And, indeed, how faint already was the memory of the king of Wildcat and his patient wife with the lacerated feet; the demented woman who had opened Dantean gates for me; the rheumatic spy who hunted "wild hawgs"; the stealer of dogs. A little new happiness — at best but an escape from sorrow — had, like a ray of sunshine, chased away the demon-peopled dark. Perhaps the dark, though, was just as real. And all because a little creature who cannot speak, and some tell us cannot reason, is with us again.

Peter, grasping the trembling Sisyphus with one hand and waving his hat with the other, stood upon the insecure seat and chanted wildly: "Farewell, Wildcat! 'And if forever, still forever fare thee well.'"

XIV

SHADY COVE

SHADY COVE! Where the sky bends low, and
mountain mists like phantom birds with white
ruffled plumage ever wing their way in and out
among recurrent rainbows that span the little valley.
Where at evening the violet of distant mountains
fades into a lilac sky, and the comforting hills
suddenly draw near to watch the Cove in its sleep.
Where at night the home lights on encircling heights
wink out one by one before the steady shine of stars,
and the tinkle of bells comes faint on the drugged
sweetness of the night breeze.

Our tent is pitched almost in the centre of the great
green bowl set so deep in sombre hills that it is like
the bottom of a well where one may see the stars by
day. And the day moon dreams through the sky as
faint as far-off music.

But Shady Cove is no unearthly benediction from the hands of the gods. It is a huge emerald cup, sweetened and drained by a river that rushes from a cave at the north of the valley, plays about under the willows with many a capricious curve and listless pause, until, remembering the message it bears, it hurries through another cavern directly south of the cave where it enters, quite as if to pretend that it had not loitered a moment in Shady Cove.

Once, they tell us, the outlet cave was choked with débris, and when a waterspout came the valley was flooded and the people went about in boats. But that was long ago. Long ago! Can it be that Time, as elsewhere, is the god here in Shady Cove! Shady Cove, as placid in the summer sun as a lost island in a tideless sea. How far away the foolishness of a League of Nations, Reparations, and Prohibition. And even burning questions of importance, as the new scale in music or Marcel Proust's place in literature!

For the one store asleep under the hackberry trees, the blacksmith shop with the mighty grapevine above the door, — a motor car has never dared the rocky hills to shriek its way through the valley, — the log church that long ago the Virginia creepers claimed, shouting each summer the praises of God and Shady Cove with all their gold-rimmed trumpets swaying in the wind, the churchyard with its flat stones above the unforgotten dead, the crouching gray farm-

houses — all rest here as indigenous as the Big Oak
which long ago Miss Mattie Porter climbed at sunset
to see "Beyant," and became a legendary character
who sought death by suicide. For Beyant to the
West and Outside to the East are "furrin" places,
certainly not worth the climbing of a tree to
glimpse.

Long ago, no doubt, women with calm faces and
steady hands tended old-fashioned flowers in their
dooryards, and swept with "bresh" brooms the very
road before their picket fences; and swept, too, their
wide, long dresses to the meetin' house without so
much as a profane shake of the dust from a ruffle.
Then, as now, men tilled the soil silently, patiently,
but never, I fancy, with the grim earnestness of other
mountain men overwhelmed in the struggle with the
stubborn earth. Then, as now, perhaps, during the
frequent showers from the ever-present diaphanous
clouds came the call of voices singing the same unforgotten songs they sing to-day. For in a shower,
when work ceases in the fields, the people of Shady
Cove seem to float together as on a sudden breeze;
and you will listen to know from which cabin comes
the sound of music.

In the dogtrot you will find a tall, cross-eyed man
with very large ears leading the singing and beating
time with the accuracy of a clock, while anyone may
be picking a banjo or bowing a fiddle. And what joy
to drift in unnoticed, quite as though we belonged,
and join in the refrains : —

Sister, look how you step on ther cross.
      Sound the jubilee!
'Cause yer foot might slip an' yer soul be lost.
      Sound the jubilee!

Or to "roodle-doodle-doodle" with them in their version of the old hunting song which perhaps their ancestors brought over from England : —

Give er whoop an' er high-low.   On er meeny stand!
An' er run, run, run, an' er tippy, tippy tun.
Away ther royal dawgs!
R-r-r-roodle-doodle-doodle an' a bugle, oh!
An' a whack-fal-daddle an' a oh, heigho!
Through ther woods we run, brave boys,
An' through ther woods we run.

or,

Far' ye well, my Dinah.
Ohoo-oo!   Ohoo-oo!   Ohoo-oo!
Gwine erway ter leave ye.
Ohoo-oo!   Ohoo-oo!   Ohoo-oo!

And how Peter, but moderately endowed with the gift of song, would throw back his head and mourn mightily for Dinah, "Ohoo-oo! Ohoo-oo! Ohoo-oo!" and John, touched by some far-off race memory, would howl in key, to everyone's satisfaction.   And how we shouted, "She 's Comin' Round the Mounting."   And how our voices sank to the sadness of hope deferred on "when she comes."   And in my ignorance I had thought it a modern radio song.

But no radio artist can ever sing it as these people whose lonely ancestors called it across the sea.

Though there is no blessing of song in the fields as in the Old South, yet Shady Cove sings with becoming nonchalance — like robins after rain. For while it may be fitting that some especially endowed songster should sing at an appointed time, while other less gifted birds perch uncomfortably about in their best preened feathers and strain their critical faculties for a false note, it is scarcely the way to saturate the being with our latest evolved gift — the sense of music. But heaven forbid that I should sully the still air of Shady Cove with a fanatical idea. Shady Cove, that takes even its religion in such a matter-of-course way that there has never been the need of a "*ree*-vival." And where every third Sabbath the minister comes from Beyant, and, like Tennyson's Northern Farmer, they "thowt a said whot a owt to 'a said," and no questions asked.

But Shady Cove has its rigid conventions. A woman, for example, must not appear on the road or at the store without a sunbonnet well tied; nor must a man engage in conversation with her except she is safe indoors. It was conceded that the greenwood tree before our tent was our castle, and thus it was understood that I could converse with anyone without a sunbonnet and under the canopy of Heaven. Our first evening in Shady Cove, as we sat by the dying camp fire in the starlight, there came the slow tread of horses' feet, and in the spectral light two troubadours approached, each playing a banjo and singing softly, but very distinctly : —

> "I 'll pray fur ye at nightfall
> Whin all ther worl' is still.
> Whin dark is on ther mounting,
> An' stairs shines on ther hill."

When we invited them to light and hitch they sang serenely on — "Far'well ter Lookout Mounting," "Barbara Allen," "Ella Ray," and "The Basket Maker's Child." Their young voices were sweet, and it was all very lovely in the starlight. And when we stirred the embers of the fire and toasted our last box of marshmallows, and all drank hot cocoa, they were sufficiently cheered to sing, with a rollicking *martelé* staccato from the banjos : —

"Up on ther mounting ter plant my sorghum cane,
  Ter make a barr'l o' 'lasses, ter sweeten Lizy Jane.
  I hain't goin' ter marry a widder. I 'll tell ye ther
    reason why :
  They hes too miny chillern thet makes ther biscuit fly."

It was late when they mounted their horses and stalked off in the shadows singing softly the old, old lullaby : —

> "Roland rocked me in his arms.
> So long — so long ago."

And we sat by the camp fire an hour relishing in our simple way the peculiar flavor of Shady Cove. And often, in the week that followed, we tried to understand this valley where the people have known each other so long — through successive generations — that Chesterfield's advice to his son, "A glance of the eye is sufficient, my boy," is superfluous for communication with each other. And still, — proud, reserved, English, where each man's cabin is his castle, — never, we thought, could Shady Cove set a common table by the roadside after Sabbath service, with the burgomaster to preside. This we had found in a foreign village not yet Americanized. And we said to ourselves that perhaps such close bonds of neighborly love could never obtain in an empire, or in so large and so heterogeneous a nation as our own. And I ventured to wonder if the silken banner of national love with its centuries-old devices might wave more loyally, and certainly more beautifully, under our stars and stripes than when it is dyed to a common color in the melting pot of our language and customs. No, there was no communistic spirit in Shady Cove; and we rejoiced. For we had been permitted to watch so many plums of the family tree, specked, as we all are, and, alas, usually ripened but on one side, — but good plums as plums go, — pressed into a mass that becomes sour and gaseous.

But Shady Cove has its heartaches: the mystery of early death; the sick, who loom important under the direct chastening hand of God; the problem of unrequited love. For nothing has been "debunked" in Shady Cove — not even love. Then, too, there is the occasional restlessness of youth and its exodus into Beyant or Outside. Old and lonely eyes that watch the road and miss the voice that will never sing again in Shady Cove. And sometimes there is a "no 'count" man who lazes round and drinks too much liquor from the still on the mountain side.

Though Shady Cove does not neighbor with Outside or Beyant, the grapevine telegraph brought the word that Peter "war a Doc." Though he persistently disclaimed the honor, the Cove considered it as but becoming modesty.

One day, the friendly storekeeper, after he had distributed the mail — as usual from his hat — and had given us our brown sugar, said, "Ole man Battenfield's purty puny. He air sick abed." We murmured our sympathy.

"I 'low, Doc, ye would n't jist step over 'n' see him?" And before Peter could reply he went on : —

"Ye know, ther ole man ter my shore knowlidge hes ben a prayin' man fur better 'n fifty yars. Now hit 's gitten round thet he air cussin' his womern. Some claims they 's hyard him. Now I 'lows thet he jist fevers up whin he cusses — effen he do cuss. They talks round lak they means ter church ther ole man ; an' a passel o' womern is settin' round thar ter-day ripresintin' ther church an' listenin' ter hyar effen he busts loose 'ith a cuss word. Course I hain't a-sayin' hit hain't right an' proper ter church er man fur cussin' his womern — lessen he air outen his haid. Ole man Battenfield air my womern's

step-pappy an' she air pow'ful het up an' grievin'.
I reckon, Doc, ye would n't jist step round ter-day
'bout ther time he 's looked fur ter cuss, — 'bout
four o'clock hit takes him theterway, — an' kinder
tell 'em ther ole man is delirium ?"

Now the storekeeper had assisted us when John
was stolen, and we had ridden into paradise on a
board on his wagon ; so about "cussin' time" we set
out for "ole man" Battenfield's.

The "passel o' womern" constituting the church
investigating committee were seated in the dogtrot
industriously piecing quilts and murmuring in
sepulchral tones tales of the dead and dying, while
listening eagerly for any sound that might come
through the open door where the sick man lay, waited
upon by his wife. Peter went at once to the patient,
who was expecting him. I could see from my chair
opposite the door a fierce, high-nosed old man with
long gray hair and burning eyes that seemed to
search the dogtrot vengefully. Peter, with a marvelous bedside manner, took the patient's pulse, looked
at his tongue, and asked the nurse questions about
the bowls of herb tea on the table. Presently he
returned to the dogtrot, followed by the meek wife.

Peter walked to the farther end of the open hall
and began impressively : "Of course, as this is not my
case, ethically I do not feel at liberty to change the
treatment. However, I should advise that you take
a basin of water, and melt in it a square of common
laundry soap — say two inches square. After it is

thoroughly dissolved, bathe the patient for ten
minutes — no more; seeing, of course, that he does
not catch cold.   In exactly half an hour take a basin
of water, — warm, but not hot, — and dissolve in it
the medicine I shall send.   Bathe him thoroughly
in this — er — lotion I shall send.   And afterward
rub well with a wet towel."

A greater physician never prescribed a bath for
Queen Caroline with more tact.

"Mary Belle! Mary Belle!" called the patient
with surprising strength. "Why n't ye change
these hyar pillars! They air hotter 'n hell!"

Silence in the dogtrot. Every ear strained. The
clock over the mantel in the sick room strikes four.
This is "cussin' time." Now or never. Then —
horror! Our worst hopes realized. As Mary Belle
bent over and changed the pillows the old man
cried : —

"Blank ye, Mary Belle! Ye air pullin' iver'
blankety har outen my blanked haid!"

Awful silence in the dogtrot. Why did not Peter
speak! I glanced at him significantly. His face
was very red and he seemed to be seized with a fit of
coughing. But he conquered it, and rising to his full
height began slowly : —

"In certain fevers like this there occurs a phenomenon that is — er — peculiar. The phenomenon
is this. The patient is obsessed by a fear that when
delirious — that is, 'outen his haid' — he may —
er — cuss. He fears the fever — say at about four

o'clock — and he fears profanity. It comes right
along with the fear of the fever. I hope I make
myself clear. As the fever rises the fear is augmented
and the patient — er — cusses. This is a very rare
though not fatal disease, and is always accompanied
by this phenomenon. This good old man knows
that he is using profane language, but in the nature
of the disease he is unable to keep from it. Such is
the phenomenon. I should advise a very sympa-
thetic attitude on the part of his nurse and of his
friends. I shall send some medicine with written
directions at once."

The patient glared triumphantly through the door;
and the church committee sat meekly with open
mouths. But Mrs. Battenfield's gaunt figure seemed
to grow taller, and she returned to her husband with a
high head. Her man was not only cleared of guilt
before God and the neighbors, but he had the
Phenotomy — the only case that had ever been
known in Shady Cove. Indeed I afterward heard
the storekeeper asked "how ole man Battenfield's
Phenotomy was gitten on," and the storekeeper
replied, rather regretfully I thought, "He air 'bout
well of it, an' not a soul ketched hit!"

Outside, I said: "Doc, I really must congratulate
you on the new method of mixing psychology with
medicine. It was weird, but convincing. But the
diagnosis? Is the poor old man very sick? And
what on earth is that medicine you prescribed?"

"I believe the old man is too irritable to be very

sick. My opinion is that he is taking a fall from grace. And I guess he has earned it. He is taking a needed rest from piety. By George, it is a strong brand of religion in Shady Cove that can inhibit a man for over fifty years! I hope the old eagle will come through it purged and refreshed."

"I don't know about being refreshed; but Mary Belle gave him dandelion tea — a quart. But your medicine?"

"Well, I saw a lot of Epsom salts at the store. We can mix it with some of our cocoa and sweeten it with your saccharine. They 'll never discover what it is."

So we went to the store and assured the storekeeper that his "womern's step-pappy" was still in the fold — and accepted a fee of two glasses of muscadine wine cool from the well. We bought the Epsom salts, which really looked quite professional when doctored and wrapped carefully into powders for Peter to take to the patient. And when he returned he reported with pride that the patient — and especially Mary Belle — was wonderfully improved.

But now we must say good-bye to Shady Cove. We broke the news to Sisyphus in the usual manner by tinkering with his wheel, while John watched in gleeful expectancy. We must climb the mountain to Beyant — where we had learned that coal mines disfigure the earth. From the first pale windflower, through all the violets, and the foxgloves, and the

wild petunias, and the galax leaves, down to the fire
pinks that flame by the river, we had watched the
pageant of the mountain summer. Since the redbud
blushed in the valley and the fringe tree waved its
silver hair on the hill, we had rejoiced with it all.
Now, too soon, the sourwood would die in red
splendor, the hickories stand in transparent gold, the
sweet gum glow with a suffused rosy light, each
separate star etched against the autumn sky; its
kinsman, the black gum, wrapped in deep maroon,
looking warm enough for winter days when only
waxen mistletoe and scarlet holly hold carnival
among the proud pines.

On the morning of our last day we climbed to the
rim of the southmost hills and, leaning against an
oak, took our last long look into the green chalice
of the valley we had learned to love. We were silent
and listened idly to the tinkle of the cowbells on the
hills. Presently Peter became aware that a bell near
us sounded insistent, erratic. Fearing some bovine
trouble, he went over the brow of the hill to investi-
gate, and in a moment called to me.

In a little clearing before a one-roomed cabin a
child of four, perhaps, played about with a cowbell
tied by a string to her shoulders. Near her was a
boy of eleven, his thin little arms industriously
wielding a hoe in a bean patch. We walked down
and said, "Howdy." "Howdy," answered the boy
in a shy, almost a sullen way, and kept on with the
hoe. But the little girl, an elf with black tangled

lashes shading eyes of Irish blue, waved her flaxen curls and jangled her bell in delight.

"May we get a drink of water?" I asked the boy.

"Yes 'm," he answered, with what I could see was perfunctory civility. "You-all enter an' take cheers. I jist brung fraish water frum ther spring."

We followed him into the cabin, and he stopped to remove the bell from the little girl.

"Are you playing you are a moo cow?" I asked, inanely, for I know that a mountain child does not play an imaginative game — in fact, seldom plays at all.

"Violy May," said the boy, "runs round an' gits lost, an' I hain't time ter hunt her. I hangs ther bell on her so 's I 'll know whar she air."

"Are you alone?" asked Peter. "Where are your father and mother?"

"Mammy air daid. Pappy works in ther coal mines Beyant. He kims back nights."

"Lookit!" cried Violy May, running to the window. "My Pappy rides down thar — plumb down ther mounting on ther mule! But my Pappy don't kim home no more." And she began to cry.

"Course he kims home!" cried the boy, frowning. "Hit er gwine ter rain. Ye kim out 'ith me an' holp bring in ther firewood." Violy May hung her head and followed him where we could see him chopping wood with an axe almost as heavy as he, and quite as high. Peter went out and took the axe.

And presently I saw them in earnest conversation as man to man.

I looked about the clean-swept room. A bed, a table, a few pots and pans by the fireplace, clothes hanging on the wall, and, on a shelf in a row, six bottles of what I knew to be moonshine. The boy came in with an armful of wood, followed by Violy May with a single stick which she was compelled to drop as she panted over the doorsill. But she lifted it bravely again and said with a smile that would have melted a heart of stone: "Hain't ye glad ye got so good un? *I* don't talk too much!" The boy gave her an adorable grin and carefully brushed the front of her clean, faded apron.

"Ye stay in now, Violy May. Hit 'll rain, an' come on cold. Don't ye play 'ith ther matches. Ther womern 'll light ther fire." And he hurried out to hoe the beans before the shower. After a while Peter came in and paced the floor angrily. But the little figure worked on in the rain. Presently Peter burst out: "*Now* what shall we do! That boy — his name is Emmet O'Day, Emmet Jeremiah — is eleven years old next week; and his father has not come home from the mines for three weeks. See those bottles of moonshine?" he cried fiercely. I meekly replied that I had counted them.

"Well, Emmet goes down to the still twice a week and gets them — he always has — so they will not guess that his father does not come home. And he showed me a big watermelon that he is saving "'cause Pappy sho likes my watermilons.' And he's afraid, I can see, that if his father does not come home someone will take him down to the Cove away from that bean patch!"

"But doesn't he like Shady Cove?" I asked stupidly.

"You don't understand!" cried Peter, stopping in his walk. "It's the place here! He'll not leave it! It is the Shady Cove blood in the boy. Why, he's got half a tree cut down for winter wood. And he has a cabbage patch; and he's going ter chop kraut! Kraut!" and Peter roared the word as if all tragic fate lay hidden therein. Then, with an apologetic smile, "I suppose you'll have to tell him he must go down to Shady Cove."

"Why me?" I asked. "It is enough that I'll have to leave Shady Cove with a lump in my throat about these waifs. Why me?"

Peter laughed. "Of course you've found the rub! You see, I promised, man to man, that I wouldn't tell," he said weakly. "But I said afterward that I couldn't promise for you."

"Well, then, the boy knows I'll tell. So why speak to him?"

"On the contrary. He said, 'Thet air all right. A womern jist follers her man.'"

"Indeed! Anyway, I'll interview Shady Cove first. Someone may know about the father."

As we left, Emmet said shyly: "Would you-all lak a peach frum the tree by ther spring? I air

aimin' ter can some.   But I got ter git some sugar.
I 'low Pappy 'll bring hit."

"We are coming back to-morrow, Emmet," I said,
"and I will bring some sugar."   Peter gave me a
look of grateful surprise.

"Why, of course," I cried, "we cannot go Beyant
and leave things in this state."

"Certainly not," sighed Peter.

When we had told the story to the storekeeper,
Peter asked : "Do you suppose the father is killed in
the coal mines?   Or has he just deserted these
children?"

"Wal, I 'low Denis O'Day air too onnery ter git
kilt.   Lak 'nuff he air gone off on a spree an' fergot
he air got iny chillern.   He air er furriner thet kim
frum Outside.   But his womern war a Witherspoon,
born an' raised in ther Cove.   She air daid; an' her
sister married a Outside man an' moved away."

"What shall we do now?" snapped Peter.

"Why, I 'll jist lock up an' go up thar an' git 'em.
All the folks 'ithout chillern hyar 'll want 'em.
They air Witherspoons."   And he went to lock the
door of the little cage that is the post office.   "Hold
on!" he cried.   "Thar air er letter thet 's ben hyar
better 'n two weeks.   Hit air backed ter Jeremiah
Emmet O'Day."

"Oh, let me have it!" I said.   "I 'll read it.   The
child probably cannot read."

"All right," grinned the postmaster of Shady Cove,
and I read aloud : —

"Dear Jeremiah,

"Yore Pappy hes married a widder womern at er coal mine thet keeps a boardin house. He hes giv in thet ye an Violy kin live ith me now. Ther widder hes a passel o childern an don want ye. As soon as iver yer uncle kin git started we air comin fur ye in ther car. We haint got no childern but ye an Violy 'll be compny fur us.

"Yore Aunt Sarah Bateman"

"Hurrah!" cried Peter.

"Lawsy!" cried the storekeeper. "Thet 's Sarey Witherspoon. An' a pow'ful good womern. They ort ter be hyar by now." And he pushed back his hat and slumped contentedly on a nail keg. "Wal, thet air settled."

"Settled for everyone but me," said Peter gloomily. "I 'll have to break the news to that boy; and it will kill him."

"Whut fur kill him? Hit air his own a'nt, hain't it?"

"Yes, but the boy is a Witherspoon. Why, he loves that bean patch like a mother. And he 's cutting winter wood; and he 's going to can peaches for his father; and he 's going to chop kraut. Kraut!"

"Uh-huh. Wal, mebby we best keep him hyar in ther Cove."

"No, we 'll have to face it."

But I do not like to recall the boy's still white face when I read a translation — a very free translation — of the letter to him. He did not cry. But presently he went outside and I saw his thin little arms about the tree he had been chopping and his face against the bark. After a while he came back and in a voice of strained cheerfulness said, "I 'low I hed er purty good chancet o' beans — an' I war goin' ter chop kraut."

"But, Emmet," I choked out, "your uncle and aunt will be so proud that you know so well how to help them!"

The boy made no answer; and Peter laid a hand on the little thin shoulder: "Buck up, old man! Tough luck. But it comes to every man. You'll be coming back here grown-up soon." And the boy's eyes lightened for an instant.

We left them at the cabin. The boy's last night was his own. And next morning a comfortable-looking woman and a man — God be praised! — with a humorous twinkle in his eye came in on the stage, having left the car Outside. We showed them at once to the cabin, the pitifully few clothes were collected, and we started down the mountain, Peter leading the old white cow which the storekeeper was to buy. Violy rode happily on her uncle's shoulder, but the boy walked with his eyes on the ground. Suddenly he ran back and returned with a gray cat. "He'd starve up thar," he said.

"Want ter take him erlong in ther car?" asked his aunt, kindly.

"No'm; I 'low he's used ter hyar."

At the store where the stage waited on its way Outside, the storekeeper came with a knife for Emmet and a box of peppermint sticks for Violy May. And all Shady Cove gathered about with so many gifts of pies and cookies and fried chicken that there seemed scarcely room for the driver and the four Witherspoons.

As the horses started with a mighty pull up the road to Outside, Peter sighed, "Well, *that's* over!"

"Yes, over for us," I answered. For I had watched a little twitching face turn south toward the mountain where a hoe lay idle in the bean patch, and the biggest watermelon saved so long would waste its sweetness in the summer sun.

"He's only eleven," said Peter comfortingly. "Children forget."

But do they? I know a woman who to this day dares not recall the mystery of a darkened room and a child's aching, inarticulate resentment at the kindly intrusion of friends.

The last sing with Shady Cove under the rainbows. The last camp fire under the stars. And at sunrise we are climbing the rocky road to Beyant — Sisyphus wheeling at every opportunity to run back to Shady Cove of indolent, happy memory; John pulling cheerfully; and we pushing in double harness, stopping often for one more glance at the green valley we shall never see again.